# Using *Language in Use*

## a teachers' guide to language work in the classroom

## Anne and Peter Doughty

Edward Arnold

ISBN: 0 7131 1897 0

## Publisher's Note

The need for this book became apparent some time after the
publication for the Schools Council of *Language in Use* and after
the Project had ended. The authors have therefore written it on
the basis of post-Project experience independently of, but with the
agreement and encouragement of, the Schools Council.

Set in 11 on 12 pt Plantin and printed in Great Britain by
Billing & Sons Limited, Guildford and London

# Contents

To the reader    v

**I Using** *Language in Use*    1

  1    What is *Language in Use*?    1

  2    Where do I begin?    5

  3    Working through a unit    10

  4    What happens next?    15

**II What the units can achieve and who they are for**    18

  5    What do the units 'teach'?    18

  6    What do pupils learn from the units?    22

  7    Can any teacher use the units?    25

  8    Which pupils can the units be used with?    30

  9    What kind of work comes out of the units?    35

**III Teacher, pupil and unit**    40

  10    Does using the units affect teacher/pupil relationships?    40

  11    What does this mean for teachers?    45

  12    What does this mean for pupils?    48

**IV Pupils' use of spoken and written English**    54

  13    Why do the units use these ways of working?    54

  14    'Talk' and 'discussion'    58

  15    The question of 'correctness': in spoken English    62

  16    The question of 'correctness': in written English    71

**V Units in the English class** 78

17     Do the units help with the teaching of literature?     78

18     Do the units offer any scope for drama work?     83

19     Do the units allow for 'personal' writing?     86

20     Can the units help with a 'thematic' approach?     90

21     Can the units help with 'reluctant' learners?     92

**VI Units across the curriculum** 98

22     Subject teachers and *Language in Use*—the problems     98

23     Subject teachers and *Language in Use*—the possibilities     104

**Postscript** 112

**Books referred to in the text** 119

**Appendix I** Reprint of Unit Index 120

**Appendix II** Reprint of units:

    (i) A3, Judging your audience     122

    (ii) F2, Man's job/woman's work     124

    (iii) A8, Words and diagrams     126

    (iv) F4, National characteristics     127

# To the reader

Over the last three years, we have worked together presenting *Language in Use* to teachers and student teachers in many different parts of the country. On these occasions, we were often asked if we would one day write down what we had said as a guide to the new ways of working with language that we had presented. This book is the result of our promise that we would.

In the discussions which took place on those occasions, we learnt much from the teachers we met; consequently, a great deal of what we have to say in these pages incorporates the thoughts and practical experience of many individual teachers. Cumulatively, this thought and experience represents a very impressive body of 'good practice', as we might call it, and we feel we have an obligation to make this good practice available to others by putting it into this book. At the same time, we were asked many questions about attitudes to language, language learning, and the use of language, questions our audiences put to us, because they felt that they needed to know much more about these things, if they were to do justice to the new ways of working with language we were presenting. What we have tried to do in this book, therefore, is to answer these questions by discussing the practical problems of working with *Language in Use*, and to draw upon all we learnt of teachers' good practice to illustrate and exemplify the solutions we offer to them. Thus we hope we have succeeded in doing justice to both the 'good practice' we wished to present and the questions about working with language that teachers most need to have answered.

Is this book, then, just a guide for those who want to use *Language in Use*? Certainly that was how we had seen it before we began, but it became progressively clearer as we proceeded with the text that what we needed to say about *Language in Use* was exactly what needed to be said about *any* kind of work with language that takes into account the pupil's own knowledge of his language, what we call his 'language for living'. The most important thing about *Language in Use* is the way in which it asks the teacher to draw upon the pupil's cumulative experience of using language to live, as his basic resource for working with language. This focus upon what pupils can do successfully with their language provides the common ground between *Language in Use* and all the other ways of using the pupil's own experience of his language as the basis for teaching and learning. *Language in Use* offers the teacher a wide choice of activities which enable him to draw upon this experience, and sets them within a framework that is based upon a coherent view of how we use language to live, but we would be the last to claim that these activities are in any sense exclusive to *Language in Use*. It is for this reason that we have been able to talk about the problems of using *Language in Use* in terms of the problems common to *every* approach which takes as its point of departure the pupil's experience of using 'language for living'.

The aim of this book, then, is to put into the hands of every teacher, whatever his particular subject or responsibilities, a guide to the ways in which the pupil's own experience of his language can be the basis for teaching and learning. At the same time, the book is a guide to the ways in which this knowledge can and should be extended and enriched, and, in particular, a guide to ways in which teachers can help to bridge the gap that exists for so many pupils between their 'language for living' and the school's requirements in 'language for learning'. In the long run, it may well make best sense to close this gap by changing the school's view of the language it regards as necessary, or appropriate, for learning, but, here and now, there are many teachers who want to narrow the gap by making this language more readily accessible to their pupils than it is at present. Whether or not they choose to draw upon *Language in Use* for the purpose, this book can be a great help to them.

Co-authors work in different ways. In our case we find it is best for one of us to write the text and for the other to provide a critical, running commentary upon it, adding, subtracting, editing and modifying as we go along. This time we decided that Anne should write the text and make use of her own experience of using *Language in Use*. For this reason, and because we dislike the impersonal feel of many books written by more than one person, the text is written in the first person, and that person is Anne Doughty. When we do use 'we', it refers either to both the authors, as in this introduction, or to human beings collectively, embracing the reader along with everyone else. This use usually occurs when we are writing about language, or learning language, as an activity confined to the human species.

As the book is a practical guide to work in the classroom we have not filled the text with continual references to the literature of the topic in question and we have not used footnotes. Serious discussion of practice, however, particularly new practice, does give rise to important issues of theory and principle but we have only enlarged upon questions of this kind where they are essential to the reader's understanding of what we have to say about the practice of working with language. In our Postscript, we suggest a small number of books which readers might turn to first if they want to find out more about these issues for themselves.

As we have already said, this book owes an enormous amount to all those teachers who participated so enthusiastically in the conferences and meetings we addressed. We thank them most sincerely and hope that they will think we have done justice to the quality of the good practice they were so ready to share with us. Finally, we wish to thank our friends Don Salter and Jill Rebbits, a lecturer in English and a teacher of physics respectively, for reading this manuscript in its first draft. It was Don who provided detailed comment and encouragement when our energies were flagging, while Jill reassured us that what we had to say about the needs of specialists, especially scientists, was both relevant and timely.

ANNE AND PETER DOUGHTY
Manchester 1974

# 1 Using *Language in Use*

## 1 What is *Language in Use*?

In October 1971, just after the publication of *Language in Use*, we were asked to take part in a Conference in Berkshire where *Language in Use* was to be introduced to a number of teachers who had not met it before. Also present at the Conference were teachers and college lecturers who had used *Language in Use* during its classroom trials in 1969–1970.

The first speaker to address the Conference was a young College of Education lecturer who had used *Language in Use* extensively, both with his own students at College and with a group of teachers of English, working at a local Teachers' Centre. The subject of his address was, 'What is *Language in Use*?', and his answer to that question was one which we have never been able to forget. He began coolly enough, describing the physical appearance and outline of 'the red book'. He sketched in the idea of the unit and the relationship of the units to each other and then he came to the point where he wanted to explain the variety of contexts in which he and his students and colleagues had used *Language in Use*. Time was growing short and he had listed situation after situation in which teachers had used the units to initiate work in their classrooms. He referred to work with electrical apprentices in Further Education courses, to remedial work with slow learners, group work with 'difficult' secondary pupils, and report writing with A-level science students. Eventually he paused for breath and said apologetically, 'I'm sorry, I've made *Language in Use* sound like "Snibbo". You know "Snibbo", you can clean your upholstery or cure your dandruff with it. But it does seem to me that if you are at all concerned with the part language plays in living and learning then you will find something in *Language in Use* that will meet, or adapt to meet your needs. And, unlike "Snibbo", it will work.'

The claim the young lecturer was making for *Language in Use* was a very broad one: he was suggesting that, wherever learning is going on, *Language in Use* could make a contribution. In a world of specialism, where a book or an object is for one purpose and one purpose only, his claim seems highly unlikely and it is proper for the reader to be sceptical of it, just as members of that audience were. Those teachers at that Conference had many questions to ask and it is

1

partly to provide a proper answer for them, and for all the other teachers at other Conferences, that we have set out to write this book, because an effective answer to those questions cannot be given in a few words.

Like all those teachers to whom we have presented *Language in Use* over the last three years, the reader will have his own questions, his doubts and difficulties, that arise from his own experience as a teacher and from the teaching situation in which he finds himself at the moment of reading this book. What we have tried to do, therefore, is to predict what those questions and doubts and difficulties might be by drawing on our experience of the questions put to us by the many teachers we have talked to: and to answer them by making use of all that they have told us of their experience of working with language, both before and after using *Language in Use*.

One thing must be said at the outset. *Language in Use* has been described by teachers as 'a new way of looking at things'. If one is going to look at something in a new way, and that something is as complex as the way in which teachers and pupils use language, both in school and outside it, then there is a great deal to say and it cannot all be said at once.

If in Chapter I, I describe how a *teacher* feels when he makes use of a unit, it does not mean that I have overlooked, or ignored, how the pupil might feel: if I talk about older pupils, I have not forgotten younger pupils; if I talk about speaking, I am not going to leave out writing; if I talk about teachers of English, I am not forgetting that many readers do not teach English, or indeed any one 'subject'. Instant answers are not very satisfactory when one is dealing with the processes by which we learn and use language, but answers there will be to the reader's questions, although they may not be found within any one section of the book.

How then should I begin? Earlier, I said that teachers have described *Language in Use* as a new way of looking at things. What is so new about it? And how can it be used in so diverse a range of situations as that young lecturer described? What gives it its 'Snibbo'-like quality?

Underlying the diversity of all the teaching situations which the lecturer referred to there was one major common factor, language. Now, it is obvious to everyone that language is used constantly by human beings in the course of their everyday activities. We use language inside our heads to think and to plan; we use language to make relationships, to work together and to share leisure. We must use language to teach, if we are teachers; and we must use language

2

to learn, if we are pupils. For most of us, using language is so 'obvious', however, that we simply take it for granted. For most of us a world without people talking to each other would take more imagining than some of the wildest creations of science fiction. It is precisely because language is so familiar, so ordinary and so intimate a part of our lives as human beings that we often remain unaware of its precise function in our actions. *Language in Use*, therefore, sets out to make us aware of the part language plays in our lives. An essential element in its design, moreover, is the idea that *awareness* of language and how we use it makes a major contribution to any growth of the pupil's ability to *use* language, for learning or for living. The units of *Language in Use* set out to develop this awareness by providing the teacher with the means by which pupils can explore their experience of language in all the forms they know. The units are usable by any teacher with any pupil, because all the pupils in our schools have language. It is this knowledge of the language which they have learnt in family and community which the teacher draws upon to work with the units in the classroom. At the same time, and certainly by the stage of secondary school, pupils also have a growing know-ledge of the language of the 'subjects' taught them at school. This knowledge of 'language for learning', learnt in the context of class-room and school, can also provide the raw material for work with the units.

It is the knowledge of his own language which the pupil brings into the classroom with him, therefore, that the 110 units mobilise in order to help the pupil develop his use of language, whether written or spoken, whether for living or for learning. They combine a coherent picture of how human beings learn language and how they use language with suggestions for work in the classroom set out in concrete terms. On the one hand, the units make use of a very wide range of ideas about language and its use. They look at the way we use language to interpret our experience of the world; and they look at the way we use language to make the relationships that are the foundation of our lives as social beings. On the other hand, the units offer a great variety of activities which will encourage pupils to talk and write, and to reflect upon the results of their talking and writing. From this point of view, *Language in Use* could be called a guide to 'good practice', because the units deliberately make extensive use of what teachers of English have discovered over the last ten to fifteen years in their search for better and better ways of encourag-ing pupils to talk and to write, and thereby to develop their power to use language effectively.

3

For those teachers who are already familiar with this 'good practice', *Language in Use* can be a powerful aid to memory and a resource for the day-to-day planning of lessons, for it relates this practice systematically to a very wide range of activities and procedures involving talking and listening, reading and writing. Faced with the pressures of the representative secondary school time-table, many teachers have found that this was for them the great value of *Language in Use*. It set down on paper what they wanted to do, but could not always find the time to work out for themselves in terms of practical sequences of lessons. Looked at in this way, then, *Language in Use* offers a store of ideas for work with language together with practical suggestions for translating them into actual lessons, so that the experienced teacher is able to use *Language in Use* as an extension of his own accumulated experience, ready to hand in an accessible form.

There is another side to 'good practice', however. For many teachers, it is not a question of remembering what is familiar, but of coming to terms with what is new and unfamiliar, and therefore disturbing, or even frightening. While this is particularly a matter of concern to teachers new to the profession, it also includes very many teachers who have been attracted by the new ways of teaching developed in the last decade but have felt very unsure of their own capacity to use these new ways and have seen little which might guide or support them if they were to try them out. *Language in Use* offers the inexperienced or the hesitant teacher both the explicit description of new ways of working and the support of a framework while he is trying them out. Moreover, once a teacher is confident in his use of these new ways of working, he is free to develop and exploit the units as he wishes to suit his own particular classroom needs.

Many young teachers have described *Language in Use* to us as their 'secret weapon' for keeping at bay the awful fear that they will be presented with a teaching situation in which they 'cannot think what to do'. At the same time, many experienced teachers have said the same, for they have found themselves in new and unfamiliar contexts for which their own tried and tested ways of working no longer seemed adequate. Changes in school organisation, the raising of the school-leaving age, integrated studies, the mixed ability class, the multi-racial class, all these have created teaching situations in which many a teacher now feels that he simply does not have the resources he needs, however experienced he may be in other ways. Perhaps I might illustrate this from my own experience. A short time after I left University with a degree in Geography, I found myself in a Secondary Modern school in south-east London. I was

4

given as my class forty-three resentful fourteen-year-olds who were then just too young to leave school at the coming Easter. In addition to teaching them Geography, I was allocated a large number of periods and given the general directive to 'Do something about their writing and spelling'. My experience of 'English' at University had involved the literary critical study of a very large number of books, a special study of the language of Chaucer, long hours of translating Beowulf and a study of dialect in my home county. Officially, therefore, I was well qualified to teach 'English' and, had I been asked to teach O-level or A-level literature, I would probably have had little difficulty, but as it was I had nothing to draw upon when it came to working with language in this context.

*Language in Use* could have been such a help, for it would have made available to me the 'good practice' of others and relieved me of the impossible burden of trying to invent both ideas *and* techniques, while learning how to cope with the problems these girls presented to me. It would have helped me to think through what it was I was trying to do and it would have given me the opportunity to learn from what others had found successful. It would have supported me until I had something of my own to offer. With the units to guide me, I could have made much more sense of the needs of those forty-three summer leavers. They did have *something* I could have used, had I known how: their extensive practical knowledge of their own language as ordinary members of a human community. Like the student, newly returned from teaching practice, who described *Language in Use* as 'a do-it-yourself survival kit for meeting the worst they can throw at you', I would have been able to do something much more constructive than the situation seemed to allow.

## 2  Where do I begin ?

Like so much in language, the meaning of this question depends to a large extent on its context. 'Where do I begin?' means one thing when a teacher finds himself with a shiny, new, red book in his hands. It means something quite different when that same teacher carries his not so shiny, new, red book into a classroom on the day when he has decided to use a particular unit with his class. We have been asked the question, 'Where do I begin?' in relation to both these contexts, so this section will look at what the teacher needs to do *before* he enters the classroom, while Section 3 follows the teacher into the classroom and explores what happens when he puts the units into practice.

*Language in Use* does not come with a set of operating instructions

5

for the user. This has certain advantages, for it means that a teacher can come to terms with the units in his own good time and in his own way. However, with all the pressures of his day-to-day work he may indefinitely postpone his intention of trying them because he does have to work out for himself how to begin. For this reason, therefore, this section suggests how a teacher can begin to make himself familiar with the units. These suggestions are based partly on my own experience of beginning to use *Language in Use* and partly on the experiences which many other teachers have since shared with me.

The first step is to put *Language in Use* on your desk. This is not such a simple-minded suggestion as it sounds. Putting a book on your desk means, first of all, *not* putting it in the cupboard, from which it may never reappear; and, secondly, it means clearing a space, allowing a book to take up the place that might otherwise be used for piles of pupils' work or any other of the innumerable pieces of paper that fill our lives as teachers.

*Language in Use* sat on my own desk for months. Despite my initial enthusiasm on the first day of term when I opened it and saw a whole range of potentially stimulating courses looking out at me, it sat there unused for months. But it did not stay *unopened*. In the occasional moments when a class was occupied with its work; in a free period, when I could not quite face another pile of notebooks; in the lunch hour; on the Saturday when it was my turn to take detention, I would read a unit, or part of a unit, and I would think about it, not consciously perhaps, but in such a way that, slowly, I became aware of what was there. What this meant was that, by the second month of term, when I came to face a serious problem involving pupils' use of written language, there was already in my mind the idea that *Language in Use* could help me to solve it. With the Unit Index, and a few quick rereads, I found a unit that related to my problem which concerned a group of girls who were doing an examination Geography course and producing written work which just did not do justice to their grasp of the subject. It seemed to me that their grasp of the concepts involved in the work was perfectly sound, but this was not reflected in the written work they were producing for me. My efforts to develop their writing by showing them what was necessary, by *telling* them what was needed, had proved quite unsuccessful. I had reached a critical point, a point where I was willing to take a risk, for to me, as to many teachers I have talked to, using ideas or methods developed by persons unknown *is* taking a risk, because it requires one to step beyond the point where one's own experience

6

ends and, initially, one has to trust someone else's judgment. What made this step possible for me was that, first, my own experience had failed to provide anything which met the needs of my geographers; and secondly, my explorations of *Language in Use* had convinced me that what the units offered was valuable, so long as I did my part by making sense of any unit I chose to use and then by adapting it to my own situation.

This process marks out the first stage in using *Language in Use*. Before I go on, however, there are one or two additional points to be made. First, it would seem that my somewhat piecemeal approach to getting to know the units was in fact a very successful strategy to adopt. One teacher I talked to at a Conference confessed to me that she had set aside a whole weekend to have a good look at *Language in Use* and, as a result, decided it really was all too difficult and quite beyond her capabilities. This was later proved to be quite untrue, when she joined a study group at a local Teachers' Centre, but a whole weekend of *Language in Use* was not really a very good idea. There is a lot to be thought about in *Language in Use*. The ideas it presents are sometimes complex, and it is not always easy to find a way of presenting them that is not taxing for the reader, so it may take time to assimilate what one has read. It does look as if hastening slowly is the best policy.

There are other reasons, too, for hastening slowly. One of the saddest stories we have heard about *Language in Use* concerned a young teacher whose enthusiasm for the units was so great that she proceeded to use a unit with a first-year class during the first week in September. It was a disaster! The unit called for working in groups and in her excitement and haste to use the units the young teacher had overlooked the important point that the pupils in her class had not met before. They had not had time to set up any of the social patterns which one finds in a class once it has been together for several weeks, for these pupils were in a new school with a new teacher and new classmates. The young teacher presented them with a situation in which they were expected to discuss, to plan, and to make decisions, when all they wanted to do at this stage was to sit quietly and size up the new situation in which they found themselves. The response was unfortunate and the young teacher vowed never to try anything new again!

What I have called the first stage of using a unit ends at the point where a teacher matches up a particular context, or a particular problem, to a particular unit in *Language in Use*. In my own case, the match was between Unit A3, 'Judging your audience' (Appendix II,

p. 122 of this volume) and a group of geographers with a writing problem. As it happens, the girls in question were sixth formers and the examination was A-level, a situation which might seem relevant to only a small number of the teachers who read this book. There are, however, two reasons why I think this example is relevant to *all* the teachers who read this book and not just to those who may at times find themselves in the context of sixth-year teaching.

Firstly, it seems to me that the problem I encountered with these girls was a problem I had met many, many times before, with every level of ability and every age group which I had taught, from nine-year-olds to University entrants, from 'A-stream' to 'slow learners'. It was the problem created by the gap between the written work expected by the school, college, or examination, and the written work which the pupil or student was able to produce. Secondly, later in this book, I shall use examples of work which I and my colleagues did subsequently using this same unit with first- and second-formers working in science, domestic science, history and biology. I hope that by tracing my own work with the sixth form, which was the first work I did with *Language in Use*, I can, at the later stage, show how the awareness I developed using the unit in one context helped me to use the unit in very different contexts. This seems to me the best way of showing the reader how a single unit can be adapted to fit a very wide range of situations.

Let me now go back to the end of the first stage, the 'matching' stage, and consider what happens next. I reread the unit A3. For me, the key idea seemed to be contained in part of the headnote at the beginning of the unit. It said:

(The unit) explores the degree to which the writer's view of his audience must strongly determine his way of writing.

My geographers appeared to have only one way of writing and, in terms of the requirements of the examination, it was an inappropriate way. If this unit could make them aware of the need to focus on their audience for what they were writing then we might get somewhere. I considered session one. The first suggestion was that:

The class works out for each of three texts in turn its intended audience. It is best done with the class working in pairs or small groups.

I accepted the idea of working in groups, but rejected the idea of using three texts, for the simple reason that I knew that I could not get the texts I might want duplicated in time. I was also concerned about how much time the whole activity might take. The suggestion which followed, however, was immediately acceptable:

When they have done this, they should select a topic, well-known to them, and each write three pieces, each one for different audiences.

We had just finished a lengthy project on the subject of pollution and the first essays had already been written. I would ask them to write on pollution again, but who should be the different audiences? The unit suggested that the audiences should be 'well differentiated', so I had to choose, from the audiences familiar to my pupils, *four* which were as different as possible. This number, 'four', represents another modification which I had already built into my plan. Whereas the unit suggested that each pupil prepare *three* short pieces, I decided that each pupil would write only *one* piece, but it would be much longer than the suggested 150 words. At the same time, I decided to have *four* working groups, and to bring the groups together to formulate their conclusions at the end of the session.

The result of all this activity was a plan in my head and four 'audiences' written on a piece of paper. They were *The Times*, the *Daily Mirror*, *Knowledge* magazine and 'a first-former'. I checked that the school library had copies of *The Times* and *Knowledge*, and I obtained some back numbers of the *Daily Mirror*. I scheduled the session for the following week when we had a triple period, a two-hour session when I could use all the time I needed.

The process which I have just described is what one teacher did in one situation, but it is representative of how any teacher can begin to use *Language in Use*. Indeed, as I found out some time later, it is closely in accord with the way in which the originators of *Language in Use* intended the units to be used.

Before we proceed into the classroom there is one last thing to be said. An important factor in any teacher's planning, whether he is using a unit or not, is the resources he can call on within his own teaching situation. Part of my own planning, described a few paragraphs ago, showed that I rejected an idea, because I knew I had not got time to duplicate the material I would have chosen. Subsequently, I had to reject other ideas in the units, because the business of getting a tape-recorder was very complicated. The important topic of resources for learning lies outside the scope of this present book, but it would seem that the idea of hastening slowly has one more thing to offer us in this section. By moving slowly, one has the chance to familiarise oneself with the available resources and to come to terms with the fact that further action may be necessary to obtain the resources which are *not* immediately available.

Stage two, the teacher's private planning, ends when he takes the unit into the classroom. The next stage, the teacher's action in the learning situation is the subject of the next section.

## 3 Working through a unit

The plan is made, the day and time decided. What happens next? There is one sense in which taking a unit into a classroom is no different from taking any other plan into a classroom. For a start, the pupils are the same, the room is the same, your capabilities as a teacher are the same and your ability to make decisions has not changed, merely because you have made some use of practice that may not be totally familiar to you. What now follows is an account of what happened when I took the unit I described in the last section into the classroom. The account is one that I have used when talking to *Language in Use* study groups at Teachers' Centres and I have been assured by these teachers that, although my account relates to the context of Geography teaching, and they are working in the context of English, or Science, or General Studies, or whatever, the 'feel' of the unit I am describing is familiar to them. It would seem that the teacher's experience of using the unit is not markedly affected by the subject context in which it is used and it is for this reason that I have commented on my own reactions to the development of the work as well as describing what actually happened.

### 'Judging your audience' with A-level geographers

My Tuesday class began in the normal way, the girls arrived in twos and threes before the bell at 2 o'clock. We exchanged news and friendly remarks. One girl had brought me a cutting that she knew would interest me and I had found a magazine that might be useful to some of the people doing Art. When we had all come together, I explained that I thought we might do something about essay writing and that I had worked out a few ideas that might help. I explained that I wanted four groups, one in each corner of the room, and that I wanted each group to produce an article on 'Pollution' for one of four audiences: *The Times*, the *Daily Mirror*, *Knowledge* magazine, and a 'first-former'.

There was an immediate response: a certain dismay when I said 'something about essay writing', a cheering up when I said 'groups',

10

which meant that they were not being asked for individual essays, and amusement and puzzlement when I named my four audiences. As they moved into the groups and rearranged the tables I realised that in setting up the work like this there was a key element in the situation which I had taken for granted; my own relationship with these girls. I had known them since they were in the second form. In that year I had taken them on their first ever field-trip and we all got soaked half-way up a mountain. For four years we had been doing things together, preparing for O-level, preparing for a visit to France, making and cataloguing our own class library and cuttings resource. The relationship was such that whatever they might think of my idea they would not reject it without giving it a fair chance. I can think of classes I have taught that would have rejected completely what I set out to do that afternoon, but, then, I would not have tried to do this with such a class. This merely underlines the point I made at the beginning of the section that, whereas elements of the unit may be new to a teacher, there is no sense in which his own experience becomes irrelevant. In fact, it can be a major contribution to the success of the whole activity.

My pupils were now engaged in talk and planning discussion. There was laughter from the *Daily Mirror* group who were trying to give pollution a lively start for their audience. I had left copies of the newspapers on my table and most groups were already consulting these. Argument was animated in *The Times* corner; the problem was which member of the group was going to act as recorder. One girl suggested that each member of the group should write the article I had requested and then the group would choose the most appropriate one. Another thought that they should share the task by producing a paragraph each. And so on.

Three things occurred to me at that point. Firstly, how my Headmistress would react, if, drawn by the sound of laughter and expecting an unsupervised class, she appeared and found prospective A-level candidates studying the *Daily Mirror*. Secondly, how she would react to the sight of a normally active member of staff standing by the window apparently doing nothing; and thirdly, how I myself was going to react if I found that, at the end of whatever period of time I chose to spend on this activity, I had not in fact achieved anything, though quite how I was to measure what I ought to achieve was not at all clear to me.

I set aside the first and third of these thoughts and concentrated on the fact that it is very difficult to 'do nothing' if you are a teacher and are present with a class. I judged that my intervention in the

11

work of the groups at this point would not be a good idea, but I wanted to be in a position to listen to what was going on without appearing to do so too obviously. I decided to rearrange the rock collection. This was a job which would keep me almost equidistant from the four groups and which required no distracting attention from me. I could tune in on each of the groups in turn, while at the same time appearing to be 'busy'.

At this point, a girl from *The Times* group came to ask me if they might go and work in the library. She explained that they had put some of their existing work on pollution into a common pool from which they could draw material for their article and found, to their dismay, that their statistical and factual material was sadly inadequate for the job. I gave them permission to go, and asked them to come back in forty minutes time so that I could review the position. When they had gone I was torn between pleasure and irritation. How many times had I told them that they must support their arguments with evidence, statistical or otherwise? Now, in the course of thirty minutes noisy, untidy argument, they had not only worked it out for themselves but had actually asked permission to go and do something about it!

I turned my attention to the 'first-former' group. The conversation had turned to a comparison of the relative horribleness of the younger brothers of two members of the group. Should I intervene? I waited, and after a moment, a third girl said, 'Well, however horrible they are, you can't expect them to understand "contamination" if you don't explain it, so what are you going to say, what *would* they understand?'. The task was resumed and the intervention was unnecessary but I thought about the two girls who had begun to discuss 'horrible brothers', when the rest of the group had turned to considering brothers and sisters as examples of the audience for which they were writing. These two girls were the members of this class whose written work was really poor. They had scraped O-level passes, and were doing A-level Geography because the school offered no alternatives to A-level work and Geography seemed rather easier to them than other subjects. The work they produced for me was often similar in style to that which they were now engaged in producing for an imaginary 'first-former'. Should I have separated these two? Should I have engineered their presence in *The Times* group? I had not intervened in the choice of group members. Basically, they were working in friendship groups, except where one group of friends had split up of their own accord when they saw that one group was going to be too large and one too small if they did not. I wondered, too, at this

12

point, if I should have allocated the 'audiences' to the groups instead of letting four girls pick up folded slips of paper from my desk. Perhaps I could rearrange the groups at a later stage or perhaps I could get one group to comment upon the effectiveness of the attempts of another group; i.e. did the *Knowledge* group think *The Times* article really convincing? If so, why? If not, why not?

At this point, *The Times* group returned from the library. Two periods had elapsed, there had been a great deal of talk and argument, consultation, disagreement, but none of the girls had, as yet, even begun to write the article required. All of the groups had decided that although I had asked for *one* piece of work from each group, a combined effort to produce one piece was just too difficult. They decided instead to choose the best article from the individual efforts of the group. Not only had the writing not begun, but it was clear to me that the girls were tired and indeed a bit frustrated. They were just as aware as I was of the enormous demands of the examination syllabus. Certainly I could not blame them if they were wondering whether this was not all a waste of time.

I decided they needed a break, so we took ten minutes off and then reassembled as a single group. The break helped, and when I asked if one girl would report the findings of each group, there was less reticence than usual in the presentation of findings. The remaining thirty minutes of the afternoon were spent reporting and commenting in open discussion, and my fears that the time had been misspent were for the most part removed. All four groups had formed a very sharp picture of their prospective audience; they had listed a large number of difficulties inherent in writing for each group; and, without any prompting from me, had made the connection between the way they themselves wrote and the fact that, however impersonal an examination may be, there *is* an audience. One part of the afternoon's work was summed up by one of the girls who had been discussing 'horrible brothers'. She was not noted for her tact or perspicacity, but what she said was, 'You know, it's no wonder I nearly failed O-level, I've been treating that wee man (the examiner) as if he were an idiot, and he can't be, can he, or he'd hardly be an examiner?'.

Before the session ended, we agreed that the articles should be written at home so that they would be available a week hence for the same session. I had a week in which to decide exactly where we went from here. How much more time could I use? Too much would present practical problems with other work plans: too little might jeopardise what I could see had already been achieved. I was profoundly grateful that the decision did not have to be made at that

13

precise moment. In the end, we used three more periods, two on the following Tuesday and one on the Friday of the same week. It took the two Tuesday periods for the groups to assess the contributions from each member and to select the one most appropriate to the audience. In some cases, one piece was chosen, but a modification was suggested so that a particular part of someone else's work could be incorporated to strengthen the whole. This was the case with the *Knowledge* group, where one girl had produced some splendid drawings and diagrams, but a better text had been provided by some-one else. We studied the final four pieces of work and discussed for nearly a period the difficulties which had been encountered in carrying out the task. These difficulties were then related to the immediate problem of writing for the audience of one—the examiner. Having focused on the examiner himself, I suggested that they take five minutes to write down their individual mental impressions of the examiner. These impressions we compared with a fair amount of amusement. Almost all of the group had formed a picture of the examiner as elderly, male, balding and dyspeptic! Equally, they agreed that his professional qualifications would involve at least a degree and probably a higher degree. They expected that he was a College or University lecturer by profession and that he probably had a long experience of teaching as well. From this they drew the conclusion that if they were to meet his expectations, they must be very much in control of what they wanted to say. 'No woolly thinking, no padding', as one girl put it. They also felt that they needed to have a particular kind of interesting, illustrative material available to support their comments. Every single girl had pointed out the need 'not to be boring'. They saw this as being the greatest problem in being an examiner and they decided that if they could avoid boring him they would stand a better chance of success. The final comment on the session came once again from 'the girl with the brother'. This time she summed up the afternoon's work:

Really, if you're in any doubt at all about the man, you'd be better to treat him like a *Times* reader, and be on the safe side, wouldn't you?

In the final session, at their own suggestion, the girls brought in the files containing their essays for that term and for part of the previous year. Working in two's, they looked at each other's work, and commented on its suitability in the light of their recent findings. In the course of this session I discovered that I now had a whole new range of ways of speaking available to me. I could say 'That's a bit *Daily*

14

*Mirror*, isn't it?', or 'Perhaps a touch of the first-former?', and be immediately understood. What the unit had done was to offer these girls a new way of viewing their work and, in the process of exploring this new way, they had found new ways of speaking to make their understanding of it available to each other. These new ways of speaking remained and did not disappear at the end of the session. The girls used them, as I did for the rest of the school year, and the change and development in their way of writing was more than I ever would have imagined possible, given the written work they had produced for me in the September.

## 4 What happens next?

A unit has been used and a particular exploration has been carried out. What happens next? For most teachers who have used *Language in Use* this was a question which simply did not arise, for using the unit generated a situation in which what to do next seemed to present itself.

There were a number of ways in which this happened. First, there were situations where using one unit presented to both teacher and pupil a whole range of ideas which they then wanted to explore more fully. One teacher, for example, used unit F2, 'Man's job/ woman's work' (see p. 124), with a group of twelve-year-olds to initiate work on the theme of 'Family'. He followed the suggestions in the first session of the unit fairly closely and found that his pupils had become very interested in the idea that language perpetuates our habitual assumptions about the world, and that we seldom question these assumptions, because they are so built into our ways of speaking that they seem to us too 'obvious' to question. As it happened, this teacher was working in a Catholic school in Belfast, only a short distance from the 'Peace Line', a barrier set up by the Army and intended to separate two groups of people, Catholic and Protestant, whose problems are only too familiar to readers in this country. In this context, this teacher decided to broaden his 'Family' theme to embrace the idea of 'community' and so he moved on to unit F3, 'Tags for people'. Using the unit as a basis, he was able to handle a potentially very dangerous situation. He was able to ask his pupils to list all the names, 'pejorative or affectionate', which they knew for both Catholics and Protestants and to consider how these labels affected their assumptions about these two groups in the community.

Another teacher who used this same unit, 'Man's job/woman's work', had found that her class of girls, all about to leave school, were so incensed by discrimination against women over jobs and

15

rates of pay that they wanted to find out more about 'Women's Lib.'. The ensuing project extended over many weeks and the teacher used both further units and items from the Stenhouse Humanities Curriculum Project to develop the idea that our language perpetuates assumptions and attitudes which we might not necessarily accept were we once to be made aware of them.

A group of pupils wanting to know more was frequently the key factor in a teacher's choice of another unit. For example, the boys who made a tape-recorded commentary of a cup-tie as part of their work on G2, 'Watching games', also produced a tape of men selling cars in a Midlands car auction. They were intrigued by the difference between their two tapes and 'ordinary' language, the language they themselves used when talking to each other. Beginning with C6, 'Intonation' and C4, 'Accent', this group entered upon a lengthy project exploring 'People using language'.

Just as a group of pupils who want to know more may lead a teacher to use further units to expand or develop a theme, so, very often, a teacher may also want to know more, and set out to use a unit or units for this specific purpose. Many teachers have told me that when they have used a unit in one learning situation, they then want to try it out in a different learning situation because they want to extend their understanding of what that unit has to offer their pupils. In my own case, I certainly did this. After the first successful use of 'Judging your audience' with eighteen-year-olds, I wanted to use the unit with younger pupils, because I felt sure that what had been relevant for eighteen-year-olds in meeting the demands of the school was just as relevant for eleven- or twelve-year-olds. At the same time, as I did not have an A-level syllabus weighing upon me, I was able to carry through a particular exploration of my own. I used both G9 and G10, 'The language of school subjects' and 'Writing up', to find out all I could about the difficulties with language for learning these pupils meet when they come into a secondary school. After my experience with the geographers, it seemed to me that this knowledge was now vital to the success of my work, for, without it, I would not be able to judge the exact nature of their difficulties and thus I would not be able to do what would best help them.

Finally, there is one way of leading on from a unit that has been used by very many teachers indeed, a move into literature of some kind, into novels, stories, plays and poems in order to develop or continue the work begun by the unit. It seems to me that this work is far too interesting and important to be compressed into the space available in this section, and consequently this theme is developed in

Chapter V, 'Units in the English class', particularly Section 17. It must, however, be pointed out that it is by no means only teachers of English who have used units to move towards literature. Any teacher who found himself working in an 'integrated' context, or outside his own subject boundary, might well find Section 17 a useful guide to how he might use units in this way.

# II What the units can achieve and who they are for

## 5 What do the units teach?

Like the question 'Where do I begin?', the meaning of this question depends on the context in which it is asked. Most of the teachers who read this book, and both of the writers, as well as many of our pupils, have been educated in the shadow of a curriculum strictly compartmentalised into subjects, with these subjects sharply subdivided into areas. For example, we can probably all understand the situation described by a young teacher who used *Language in Use* on teaching practice in a boys' Secondary Modern in a big city:

> The boys did not seem to know that English was a language that we spoke. They thought it was a subject divided up into Poetry, Reading and Grammar.

Teachers familiar with this kind of division will also be familiar with the idea that subjects or topics are 'done', and until the pupil has 'done' them he cannot be supposed to know anything about them. Perhaps this idea is best summed up by the American College teachers Postman and Weingartner. (See p. 118.) They have developed a notion which they call the Vaccination Theory of Education:

> English is not history and history is not science and science is not art and art is not music, and art and music are minor subjects and English, history and science major subjects, and a subject is something you 'take' and, when you have taken it, you have 'had' it, and if you have 'had' it, you are immune and need not take it again.

Now both these ideas are important to us, because either, or both, of them may lie behind the question when a teacher asks 'What do the units teach?'. A teacher may well hope for an answer like, 'These units teach "X", where "X" is a readily recognisable slot in the curriculum, like English or History or Science, or a labelled space on a timetable like "Friday 5, Grammar".'

So let us try to answer the question, 'What do the units "teach"?', for this particular teacher. The short answer is that the units do not work like this. *Language in Use* takes its point of departure from the fact that we all use language, in an enormous range of different contexts in the course of our ordinary, everyday lives. In school, pupils

18

and teachers use language for learning and for teaching, for conversation and for control, formally and informally, in every classroom and in the corridors and other areas of the school territory. Language is our basic tool for thinking and learning and these activities are certainly not confined to any one period in the timetable or any one slot in the curriculum. This means that it is impossible to pin down the units and say that they teach this bit of the curriculum and no other, or that they can be assigned to some familiar label like 'Grammar' or 'English'. This really will not work, because *Language in Use* is concerned with how we use language, and language will not let itself be divided up to fit inside the compartments of the curriculum.

Having said all this, however, the problem is still there for the teacher who has the anxiety of working in a situation where things can only be done if they can be given appropriate labels. For him, a different kind of answer is necessary. In Section 3, the reader may remember that I described a bad moment I experienced while working through my first unit. At a particular point, the group who were working on the *Daily Mirror* were very lively, because they were struck by the novelty of trying to use the language of the *Daily Mirror* in a school context, and I visualised the entry of my Headmistress and her subsequent demand for an explanation. At that moment I would have much appreciated an answer to the question, 'What do the units "teach"?'.

I did not have an answer then, but now that I have had time to think, and time to explore the units, I see that the kind of answer I imagined might be possible just does not fit at all with the way the units function. Ultimately, the only kind of answer that I can give to the question is an answer in terms of language learning—that the units *teach* pupils ways in which they can learn how to bring to bear upon the problem in hand all the resources, and the resourcefulness, they possess as competent speakers of their mother tongue. In other words, pupils learn from the units how to develop, extend and exploit their knowledge of their language in relation to new and unfamiliar ways of speaking and writing, including all those new and unfamiliar ways the divisions of the curriculum present to them as they work through school.

There is an important sense, however, in which the units do not 'teach' at all. It would be much more accurate to say that they create situations in which pupils can learn. Some teachers find this way of putting things rather strange, so I shall try to explain exactly what I mean. Some time ago I was asked to talk to a group of mature students about the work I had been doing. I chose as the title for my talk, 'The language needs of learners', and because the students I was talking to were going to teach a variety of secondary subjects I tried to use examples of language difficulties in a variety of subjects. The session went well and subsequent questions and discussions were interesting and lively. After some time had passed, an older woman rose to her feet. She commented that she found what I had to say most interesting, but found *my* language rather strange. Why, for example, did I talk about 'learners', when I meant 'pupils'; about 'learning situation', when I meant 'classrooms'; and about 'asking pupils to do things', when I meant 'telling pupils to do things'? What her question implied was that I was using new terms for old ideas. In effect, I was not. We have two words in English to describe those undergoing formal education, 'pupil' and 'student', but are these the only people who are learning? My three-year-old neighbour is certainly learning when she reads 'Harry, the dirty dog' with me, but is she a 'pupil', and does the big chair in the living room constitute a 'classroom'? Is there a difference between 'asking' her to read with me and 'telling' her to do so?

What I have tried to illustrate in the last paragraph is the idea that, if we come to see things differently, then we have to find new ways of speaking to show that this is the case. 'Learner' is a word that can be used of any person, regardless of age, who is doing something new, whether that learner is a pupil in school, a mature student at college, or a senior citizen taking up a new leisure activity, and a 'learning situation' can be the bed of a stream where my pupils are measuring the size of boulders or the factory bench where an apprentice works.

So let me return to the point where I said that there is one sense in which the units do not 'teach' at all; and that it would be much more accurate to say they create situations in which pupils can learn. What lies behind this sentence is not 'new words' or 'educational jargon', but new ideas. Firstly, the idea that pupils can learn more effectively if their own capacities and curiosities are fully engaged than if they are relatively passive recipients of information. Secondly, there is the idea that there are educational advantages to be gained by making the boundaries between subjects less rigid and by seeing that one great unifying force in the curriculum is the fact that we must all use language to achieve our ends, pupils and teachers alike.

Let us look at just one unit and see how these ideas can be related to it. The unit is A8, 'Words and diagrams' (Appendix II, p. 126). 'Words and diagrams' is concerned:

with the relationship between diagrams and the language which is used to explain or supplement them.

What does it 'teach'? It doesn't. It creates a situation where pupils come to see the problems which arise when you try to do certain jobs either by using words only or by using a diagram only. At the end of working with the unit, it could be that some pupils have learnt to wire a plug, to change the film in a camera, or to set up a tape-recorder, but these are, in fact, only examples of the activities a teacher might use in exploring this topic. What the pupil will have done is to explore for himself, and in his own terms, the relationship between words and diagrams, just as my geographers explored the relationship between text and audience. Like them, therefore, this pupil will carry away from the work a capacity which can be used not only in the Science laboratory or the Domestic Science room, but in any context where words and diagrams go together. The teacher has not 'taught' a pupil how to set up and describe a scientific experiment, or how to pin a paper pattern, but he has created a situation where the pupil himself has learnt what underlies the possibility of doing these activities successfully, and such activities are certainly not confined to one room in the school, nor indeed, to the school itself.

The teacher has not 'taught', but he has 'caused to happen', and he has 'caused to happen' by deploying his skill, judgment and experience in using the unit to create a context in which language learning can take place. The part of the teacher was just as critical in creating the new learning situation in which pupils made these explorations as it was in presenting information in the old and more familiar type of situation. In this new situation, however, what the teacher has to focus on is not what the units teach, but how they make it possible for his pupils to learn.

This section has moved from the question, 'What do the units "teach"?', to the question, 'What do pupils learn from the units?'. This movement, or change of perspective, represents a change in educational thinking which many teachers are aware of, but may not themselves have directly experienced. *Language in Use* is one expression of this kind of change. What this and the next chapter will do is to describe as fully as possible what these changes imply for teachers and pupils so that the reader can work out for himself how these changes would affect his own teaching situation.

What remains to be said here is that, whatever may be the case for other aspects of the curriculum, the change in perspective is absolutely vital for the successful development of pupils' ability to use their mother tongue in speaking and writing, because that is the one aspect of the curriculum where we can be sure that the pupils before us possess already a knowledge of the subject far greater than any we will ever be able to give them. It is for this reason that the ways of working in the classroom associated with this change of perspective play so large a part in the suggestions that the units contain.

## 6 What do pupils learn from the units?

As I suggested in the previous section, the units themselves do not provide the raw material for lessons in the way that the traditional textbook does. They provide the *teacher* with the means of creating sequences of lessons in which pupils can provide the raw material for learning in the shape of their existing knowledge of the language. If this is the case, then it is reasonable to ask, 'What *do* pupils learn?'.

In the simplest terms, he learns how to use his language more effectively by using it over a range of situations he might not otherwise encounter. Now 'learning how to' is rather different from 'learning' and I must make this distinction clear. If, for example, one asks people what they learnt at school, they will often say, 'I learnt History and Geography and Science and Mathematics, and I also learnt how to swim and how to play football'. There are many people who would feel uneasy about saying, 'I learnt swimming' or 'I learnt football' and behind an uneasiness of this kind there is usually a good intuition about the way the language shapes meaning for us. The same people, for instance, would be happy to say 'I played football', but not, again, 'I played swimming'. What then is the difference between 'Learning History' and 'Learning how to swim' and why, when one might possibly say 'Learning swimming', would one never say 'Learning how to History'?

What I would suggest is that the form of words used reveals a difference in the kind of activity which is going on. 'History' represents a coherent and organised body of knowledge 'out there'. It exists independently of each one of us. It is a body of knowledge which it is possible to talk about acquiring or learning, while swimming is an activity, a way in which the human body can be taught to function with a little practice, providing there are no physical or psychological difficulties impeding it. Now when we talk about a pupil 'learning from the units', as a result of his activities in the learning situation which has been created by his teacher with the help of the units, we are talking about a 'how to' kind of learning. Though we can talk about human beings 'learning language' we do not 'learn language' as we may 'learn History', because language is both a something 'out there' which the very young child does have to learn, and, once learnt a something 'in here', an intimate part of every individual human being. For the pupil, therefore, language is something of which he has a very extensive and intimate knowledge and which he uses constantly and successfully for the business of living. It is so much a part of him that he thinks no more about his ability to use language than he does about his ability to walk upright.

If pupils are using language successfully as part of the ordinary everyday business of living, what then have they to learn? Why is it that they seem to be so inadequately provided once they get inside school? Firstly, unless a pupil's knowledge of language has been exceptionally extensive, it is highly unlikely that his knowledge will enable him to use language in all the ways that are expected of him in the context of school and learning. Secondly, one can have a very extensive knowledge *of* something and still not know how to make use of that knowledge in a particular situation. Think of the highly competent car driver trying to find words to explain the workings of a clutch to someone beginning to learn how to drive. Think of a very experienced teacher, accustomed to classes of above average ability, faced with using his knowledge *of* teaching in the new context of a class of very mixed ability.

What the units do is to provide the context in which pupils can make use of their existing knowledge of language and, by using that knowledge, by drawing upon the resources provided by the teacher, by pursuing the activities suggested by the units, they can develop a new awareness of their own capacity to use language in such a way that they develop also an understanding of the possibilities of new ways of using language. So often, what limits pupils is not their lack of knowledge *of* the language, but their lack of understanding as to how that knowledge might be used.

Let me refer once more to Chapter I, Sections 3 and 4, and consider how this view of the pupils' needs can apply to the group of geographers whose work with 'Judging your audience' I described there. First, the girls, at eighteen, certainly had an extensive knowledge of their own language. This knowledge they brought to bear upon both the resources provided, in this case newspapers and magazines, and upon the tasks which I asked them to perform, organising themselves as a working group and then writing for four very different audiences. What they did in the course of the six periods we used was to make some of their intuitions about language more explicit both to themselves and to each other. They also carried their thinking well beyond their intuitions, however, because the task in which they were involved raised certain questions about the relationship between writer and audience, context and a reader's expectations. These questions they were able to answer, from their own resources, and from the information that revealed itself in the course of their working discussions, because they were given enough time to carry out their exploration at a pace that matched their thinking. In the course of this unit, these girls learnt how to assess an audience in terms of its assumptions about the world, its expectations of the writer, and its probable prior knowledge of the topic. They were also able to explore the nature of the difficulties different audiences present and what effect these differences can have on the wording of the text.

Is this all that they learnt, however? Growth of awareness such as this is a very important part of what any unit is trying to achieve, but there is another side to the unit as well. If pupils are to develop effective ways of speaking and writing, then they must have practice in these activities. Any adult knows that you become a good driver/ knitter/speech-maker/carpenter, or whatever, by spending time driving, knitting, making speeches or doing woodwork. Using language is no different from these other human activities in this respect. We can only speak or write effectively in proportion to the opportunities we have to practice speaking or writing, and awareness alone will not develop a pupil's capacity to do either of these. It is for this reason that every unit suggests a variety of writing and speaking activities, ranging from script-writing, tape-recording, planning by discussion, decision-making, acting, to questioning, collecting, analysing and reporting. With the majority of units, it is also possible to have personal and imaginative writing of many kinds emerging from the work, if this is what the teacher wishes. Through these activities pupils gain the opportunity to use language in many different ways, while, at the same time, the activities themselves are furthering an exploration which leads to the growth of their awareness as to what is implied by using language in these ways. This growth of awareness is what enables pupils to assess what they have been doing and to decide how effective their speaking or writing has been for the situation in which they have been called upon to speak or write.

What we have in the unit is a two-way process. The development of awareness which results from the explorations pupils undertake, puts the pupil in a position to review and comment on what he does, while the actual *doing*, whether it is speaking or writing, develops his capacity to handle his own language. At the end of the last section, I suggested that 'what was learnt' from the unit on 'Words and Diagrams' might vary from the ability to 'Set up and describe a scientific experiment' to the ability to 'Pin a paper pattern'. Similarly, in this section, I can say that the capacity any one unit might develop could vary from the writing up of a balanced report to the tape-recording of a discussion of a poem entirely monitored by the group themselves. Perhaps it needs to be said that one of the most difficult things pupils have to learn when they are asked to work in groups is how to exercise control over each other so that all can contribute and the task be accomplished. This is a way of using language every bit as important as the writing of a balanced report.

All these things, however valuable they may be in themselves, and necessary as they may be to the work of any particular teacher, do not themselves constitute the end product of a unit. They are all local instances of the means by which pupils can grow in their experience of using language. What is important to the pupil is not what he has done on any one occasion. The geographers had not learnt how to write for *The Times* or the *Daily Mirror*. They had not learnt how to write for one specific audience. Ultimately, what they carried away from those sessions was a vastly sharpened intuition about the need to match the language one uses to the context in which one is called upon to use it. Included in this was the vital understanding that, in order to be *able* to do this matching success-fully, one has to be able to 'read' the context and use the information it yields as a guide to the language one chooses to use. As one of them saw in her comment on her own work, if you misread the context you are sure to choose the wrong way of speaking or writing. In other words, if your awareness is not adequate to reading accurately the situation you find yourself in, whatever your competence in speaking or writing, your choice will not meet your needs; conversely, even if you read accurately, lack of practice or experience in using the relevant way of speaking or writing will mean that you fail to say or write what you would wish to say or write. What the units provide is a context in which pupils can pursue both these ends in a proper inter-relationship with each other.

# 7  Can any teacher use the units?

The units in *Language in Use* are written in such a way that they can indeed be used by any teacher. There is no technical language in a unit specific to any one group of teachers and there are no activities or procedures used in the units which a teacher might find unfamiliar,

25

because they belong to one specific area of the curriculum. Given that every teacher requires pupils both to speak and to write, and that the aim of the units is to develop these capacities for both teacher and pupil, it would certainly seem that using the units could be of advantage to any teacher. In practice, however, it does not work out quite like this. There are some teachers whose view of teaching and learning is such that they have very great difficulty in coming to terms with the ways of working which the units require. There are also some teaching situations which so tightly constrain those who have to work in them that using the units presents special difficulties.

Let me consider, first, the situation of those teachers who experience difficulty in coming to terms with the units, because their view of teachers and pupils, and how they should relate to each other, is very different from the view implicit in the design of the units.

An incident I have already used in this chapter will show what I mean by this kind of difficulty. In Section 5, page 20, when I was looking at the relationship between new words and new ideas, I recalled an occasion when a mature student questioned me on my 'strange' use of language. One of the points she made was that I always said, '*Ask* the class', when I meant, '*Tell* the class'. What I had said was what I had meant, but the question she put to me revealed her unease, not with my words, but with my *meanings*. There is all the difference in the world between *asking* and *telling* when one is thinking in terms of personal relationships. What this woman demonstrated very clearly in her response was the profound uneasiness many teachers experience when they realise that using the units implies a change in their relationship with their pupils, and, consequently, in their attitude towards them as learners. Much more will be said about this subject in Chapter III, but I would like to add a further illustration at this point to show how taxing a problem the units can present to teachers who find themselves in this situation.

Two years ago the writers spent a week in Belfast working with a group of teachers who were studying *Language in Use*. The teachers were all interesting and thoughtful people who had given up a week of their summer holiday to attend the course. Discussion was lively and only one or two people remained silent. Towards the end of the week, one of these few, silent teachers came to me and said, 'I've thought about what you've both been saying, and I think you're right. I can see you're right about developing their language, but, you see, I teach in a very difficult school and I keep order by a mixture of toughness and being fair—if I were to use the units I'd have to change my whole way of going.'

We were very much impressed by what this teacher had to say. He worked in the most uncompromising of situations in a 'tough' boys Secondary Modern in one of the most battle-scarred areas of Belfast. He was as near to being 'well liked' as is possible in a school where so many boys are embittered and alienated from the whole idea of 'school', and he was brave enough to admit that, at that point in time, to do what he now accepted was necessary would be beyond him. Teachers who can recognise their own situation in what our friend from Belfast said may want to use the units, but whether they do or not may well depend on the kind of help and support they can find, either in their own teaching situation or through the local Teachers' Centre. Some teachers have said that it was working with the units themselves that actually helped them to make these changes in their own 'way of going'; once they had made the initial effort to start using the units, they saw that they could move at their own pace, and this was itself encouragement enough for them to continue. Others have said that the key to their overcoming their own fears was the chance to share the work with others and gain support through talking out their problems at the initial stage with other teachers who were also making the attempt to use the units. Once again, many have said how valuable they have found the support of a *Language in Use* study group at their local Teachers' Centre for this sharing of ideas and problems.

A second group of teachers who may find great difficulty using the units are those teachers who try to treat the units as subject-matter to be taught. For example, when I lent my own copy of *Language in Use* to my colleague, the Head of English, a highly qualified teacher with over thirty years' experience, she returned it to me with the comment, 'Yes, very interesting indeed, but I could never *teach* all that *and* the syllabus'. The idea of a *resource*, which she could draw upon at need, was quite alien to her conception of what it was to teach. The units could only appear to her as another course book to be worked through from beginning to end. What was even more difficult for her was the idea that pupils *do* have knowledge they have not actually been *taught* in school which one can draw upon in one's teaching. She found it impossible to accept the fact that when one works with pupils' language in school, this work must necessarily relate to what they have learnt to do with language outside school.

This point leads me to mention a third group of teachers who may underestimate the potential of the units, because they do not really believe that pupils have that untapped knowledge of their language and how to use it which the units depend upon. These teachers do not accept that linguistic failure plays any part in the educational failure of their pupils. They assume that pupils are 'stupid', 'unintelligent' or 'lazy', because they 'can't write', or 'can't spell', or 'can't put a simple sentence together': and that, consequently, there is nothing to be done about this weakness. Having made this estimation of their pupil's capabilities, they judge that the units are only suited to 'the more able' or 'the grammar streams', because they require from pupils the sort of language activity of which they are quite sure their own pupils are incapable. With all three groups of teachers, it has to be said, therefore, that some change in individual practice would have to happen were they to use the units. Such a change is a matter that no one should decide for another. It is up to each teacher to decide for himself whether changing his practice is a price worth paying for the resulting gain in his pupils' ability to use their own language for living and for learning.

I have just considered how the teacher's individual practice can affect the using of the units but what must also be considered is how the teaching situation itself can affect or prevent the using of the units even when a teacher is willing and anxious to use them. It is not possible to give a complete list of difficulties created by teaching situations, but the following examples will help the reader to see the sort of situation which might create local difficulties for him in using the units.

Firstly, many units can be used successfully only when a teacher has built up a relationship with the class. This means that teachers who do not have classes regularly, or who have the kind of absenteeism that makes class composition irregular, may not be able to use these units. On the other hand, some teachers have found that it is precisely in this situation that the units are so useful, because they can provide a framework for continuity. Secondly, a teacher may find himself with a class who are very unwilling to say anything. If a class sits in silence, then a teacher is seriously handicapped, because he is deprived of the raw material he needs for his work with the units. Unless there is a minimum response which the pupils can bring to the situation, it is not possible to initiate the exploration of any topic. The problem of silence can occur in very strangely contrasting situations, however. Consider, for example, the following two comments. The teacher of a scholarship class at a London grammar school reported the complete failure of her attempts to use the units. 'Basically', she wrote, 'the trouble seems to be that the units assume a knowledge of the outside world, and these girls spend such a proportion of their time studying, either at home or at school, that they have virtually nothing to bring when it comes to knowledge of the world.'

In contrast, here is a report from a teacher working in the Secondary Modern school in a small town in rural Northern Ireland:

Teachers in a school like ours face certain difficulties peculiar to our situation when we attempt to use material like *Language in Use*. None of the pupils possess technical equipment such as tape-recorders, some houses do not have TV, nor take a daily paper, books not in the school library must be borrowed from the county library 25 miles away. Our pupils are not as sophisticated at 15 as city children, the uniformity of their background, religion, upbringing etc. means they are unaware of many of the tensions of modern life.

This report was written in 1969 and since then the town in question has become only too aware of some of the tensions of modern life, but the situation encountered by this teacher has some features in common with what teachers have reported from other rural areas. For completely different reasons, these two groups of pupils could not, in fact, make the contribution which many units require of them, because their experience of the world has been so limited. There are certainly units which could be, and indeed were, used in these situations, but it is fair to point out that even greater skill in choosing the unit to suit the class is required of the teachers who have this kind of difficulty to contend with.

There is more to say on the subject of pupils' reactions to the work required by the units in Section 8, but what I must look at now is the way in which pupils' basic *attitudes* can create situations in which there is difficulty in using the units. Once again, I will give two contrasting examples to show what I mean. In the first situation, a young teacher was working with fifteen-year-old boys in a Secondary Modern school in the North of England. He had already established a friendly relationship with the boys in the course of reading stories and poems with them. He then tried to initiate a class discussion on a topic of burning local interest, the transfer of the star player, a local boy, from one Cup team, strongly supported in the area, to another and rival team. His initiative was met with complete silence and eventually he gave up his attempt. Fortunately, he recounted his experience to an older teacher who had worked in the area for many years. This teacher had some idea what the trouble might be, and, having made discreet enquiries, he was able to explain that when the young teacher asked individual boys to express an opinion, they thought they were being 'picked on'. They chose silence as their best defence. The attitudes towards talk and discussion present in a community may well affect the individual in his work with the units, for it is the attitudes of the community which pupils bring with them to school.

In the above example, the community and its values have created a difficult situation for the teacher. Unfortunately, it is not only the community which can do this. The school itself is often responsible for the silence of pupils. A young teacher on her first teaching practice had got to know one of her classes quite well, so she thought she would try to develop a discussion with them. Unfortunately, they remained quite unresponsive to her efforts and she had to abandon the idea. It took the student some time to discover the reasons for her 'failure'. She 'observed' lessons given by other members of staff in the school and what she found was that in no class was a pupil ever asked to produce anything other than a one word answer to a Yes/No type of question which the teacher asked. Invariably, the one word answer was either 'right' or 'wrong'. What the student-teacher had done was, firstly, to make a demand upon her pupils' capacity to use language which they could not possibly meet, given their opportunities to practice and the 'public' context of class discussion; and, secondly, she had put the class in the impossible position of having to decide what a 'right' answer was in the context of an invitation to 'Discuss'. Not surprisingly, the class could not cope and once again chose silence as the surest defence against a challenge they felt they could not meet.

How a teacher might try to cope with this kind of silence will be taken up in Section 8, 'Which pupils can the units be used with?'. From what I have said in the foregoing paragraph it will be clear to the reader that an answer to this question will not simply be a matter of discussing 'age and ability'. The 'responsiveness' of pupils, which appears here as a major factor in deciding who can use the units and in what situation, continues to provide a focus for discussion in the next section where the emphasis shifts from teacher to pupil.

## 8  Which pupils can the units be used with?

Whenever teachers ask this question, they usually expect an answer in terms of a particular age-group and a particular level of ability, because teachers are so familiar with the whole range of 'graded' materials, graded either in terms of age or ability. Once

30

again, I have to say that *Language in Use* just does not fit this pattern. We have ourselves seen the same unit used successfully with first-year secondary pupils and College of Education students. Taken as a whole, *Language in Use* has been used with junior as well as secondary pupils, day release students in the College of Further Education, students in Colleges of Education and post-graduate students working for the Certificate of Education. As regards ability, the units have been used with children with IQ ratings of 70, with Newsom and RoSLA groups, with adult illiterates, with pupils in Community homes, with A-streams in comprehensive schools and with graduate science students. There may well be other groups using *Language in Use*, but these are some of the groups we have observed, or know about personally, and they certainly do provide a very wide range of age and ability.

It is, indeed, somewhat unusual for materials to have this kind of range of applicability, but there are two very good reasons why the units should be like this. Firstly, *Language in Use* is written for teachers and *not* for pupils. This means that a unit is very flexible. A teacher can use what it offers in his own context by making the appropriate adaptation. The unit is a plan for a sequence of lessons. It gives the teacher a clear idea of what work is involved and how it can be carried out, but the unit does not lay down rigid rules. It is left to the individual teacher, who alone knows the needs of his class at that moment in time, to decide how best he can use the suggested programme of work in the unit with that particular group on that particular day. What the unit offers, therefore, is a series of concrete suggestions for work in relation to a specific topic, but the suggestions leave the individual teacher free to interpret them as he needs according to the particular demands of his own teaching situation. It is this feature of the unit that gives its very wide range of applicability, considering differences of age, of ability, and of teaching situation.

For example, just as it is perfectly reasonable for a teacher to use a Ted Hughes poem with eleven-year-olds and with sixteen-year-olds and to suit his comments and questions to the age and experience of the classes, so 'Family Names' can be used equally well by Junior or Secondary pupils. Certainly a poem or topic can be difficult in itself, but what so often creates difficulty for the pupil is not *what* he is asked to study, but *how* he is asked to do it. In particular a critical question for him is what he is asked to *say* about the matter in hand, and what form of an answer his teacher will be prepared to accept. The units leave open to the individual decision of the teacher what level of 'difficulty' he will impose in the way he sets up the work with

31

the unit in his own class-room. For instance, had those geographers in Chapter I been asked to make a formal and stylistic comment on the goodness or badness of the language used in the newspapers they took as models, it is unlikely that much would have been achieved. The effort of finding words to say which would have satisfied this demand would have left nothing over for conducting the exploration. Left to find their own terms, they did comment on the differences, but *as a result of their enquiry*. What they said was a product of work done, not a matter of using a way of speaking selected independently of their ability to handle it.

Secondly, *Language in Use* is concerned with language, and language is used by human beings of every age and ability. If the materials are focused on something which every individual has and uses every day of his life; and if they are allowed to make use of this knowledge in the process of their work with the unit; and if what they bring to this work is accepted as valid by their teacher, because it arises out of their cumulative experience of using language as ordinary human beings; then *all* pupils, whatever their age or ability, will have something to contribute to the work of a unit, and hence there will be something that they can gain by pursuing it. The critical thing here is that the teacher should not have too rigidly formulated an idea of what *he* wants pupils to get out of a unit. He must know where he wants to start, but he cannot know where he will end, until he has seen what his pupils bring him in the course of their work with the unit.

So, when we ask 'Which pupils can the units be used with?' the answer is that any pupils can use and benefit from them, given that their teacher adopts an appropriately flexible approach in adapting the units to meet their needs. Whether or not the pupil with whom the unit is used is able to benefit from the experience depends very largely on the skill of the teacher and the difficulties or advantages of the teaching situation in which that teacher works, and in this the units are no different from any other source of learning in the classroom.

In the last section we looked at two examples of situations in which pupils were handicapped in their response to the units by their limited knowledge of the outside world. We also saw how two groups of pupils were unable to respond to the units at all, because the attitudes they had acquired from their community or from the school prevented them from making a free use of their everyday command of language in the context of the classroom.

Does this then mean that the old criterion of 'age and ability' has been replaced by a degree of 'responsiveness' which must be present before a unit can be used with any group of pupils? In one sense, the answer to this question is 'Yes'. Without a certain responsiveness from a class, both a willingness to offer experience, and a willingness to engage in the difficult task of putting it into words, it is true that some of the units in *Language in Use* could not be used. But, and this is a very important 'but', the units do provide a teacher with ways of building up this very responsiveness which he needs. As this is not immediately obvious from a first examination of the units, I shall show what I mean by going back to the 'silent' examples of the last Section (pp. 28 and 29) and contrast these with the work of another teacher where things turned out rather differently.

Let us consider the fifteen-year-old boys in the North of England school who failed to 'discuss', because they thought they were 'being picked on'. Working in a very similar situation, another young teacher decided that the important thing was to get 'talking in class' accepted as a normal activity with his pupils before he attempted a whole-class discussion. He decided to modify unit A4, 'Reporting events', to meet his requirements because the main interest of his group of fifteen-year-olds was football. Firstly, he organised a class outing to a major national football event and then he asked the class to collect as many newspaper reports of the match as possible. On the following Monday morning he had little difficulty in initiating a discussion of the match with the boys. There were a number of reasons for this. Firstly, he asked the boys to work in groups, reading the newspaper reports they had collected, and discussing them prior to writing their own reports. The small group situation was much less formal than the whole class situation which I described in the last section, the situation in which both teachers failed in their attempt to initiate discussion. Secondly, the boys had had a period of time in which to think through their experience of the match and they were consequently more ready to express an opinion. Thirdly, their interest and enthusiasm was aroused by the way in which different newspapers reported the events they themselves had witnessed. This interest overcame the reticence which they might otherwise have experienced at speaking in class.

By using this way of working, the teacher was able to create in his classroom an atmosphere quite different from that of the rest of the school where these boys were accustomed to producing only one word answers or nothing at all. Using this approach, the teacher gave his pupils time to get used to the idea that they might talk; that they might have an opinion to offer, or a disagreement to voice; that they might have to explain, or to analyse or to report. Despite the fact that considerable demands were being made upon their ability to handle both spoken and written language, these boys did not revert to the silence which defeated the teachers in the last section, partly because they had gained confidence in the small group situation, and partly because the teacher created situations where they were both interested and engaged in what they were doing. By using a unit which broke down the whole class situation into small groups and which provided an interesting focus for activity, the teacher was able to develop the responsiveness he needed to be able to draw upon if he was to make whole class discussion possible.

There is not space in this section to give further examples of how very different groups like electrical apprentices or remedial pupils used the units, but examples of this kind will appear in later sections of the book, and demonstrate further the point I have made about the very wide range of applicability which the units have. What I would like to do with the space remaining in this section is to take up one single aspect of how a very wide range of pupils might benefit from the units.

Very many teachers are concerned about the lack of self-confidence which they see in many of their pupils. Often, this situation is a product of the school itself, for whereas most schools point out regularly what the pupil has failed to do, only some spend time pointing out what he has done successfully. In this situation, a teacher may meet the sort of demoralised class who say, 'Oh, we're no good, we're B's or C's or D's' or 'We can't write', or 'We don't know anything', or 'Mr X calls us "Woodentops" '. In a situation like this the units can do a great deal to help, for they provide opportunities for pupils to contribute by bringing to the work what they *do* know. I quickly discovered in my own work that there were many units which could be used specifically to focus pupils' attention upon what they did know. For example, I asked a demoralised fifth form to write about 'Glaciation' for the second form. This was an idea I had developed from my earlier work with 'Judging your audience' which I described in Chapter I. What this way of working did was to enable the fifth form to see just what they had achieved in their studies by putting them in a position where they had to compare what they themselves knew with what the second form might know. The effect on morale was such that even had nothing else been achieved, though they did in fact produce some very good pieces of writing, I would have been satisfied with the way the time had been spent.

34

## 9 What kind of work comes out of the units?

For all the changes in education over the last twenty years in Britain, there are still a very large number of teachers who work in situations where pupils' progress is measured by columns of marks in mark books, rows of grades on report cards, and grades or stars on folders or files of written work. In teaching situations such as these, tests and examinations are familiar and frequent, and 'exercises' are done both in class and for homework. Young teachers working in this sort of teaching situation have the problem of predicting their work with a class for weeks ahead and producing detailed notes as to work done and standards reached. When teachers with this sort of background ask, 'What kind of work comes out of the units?', in effect, they are asking a question about how they can use *Language in Use* and still meet the necessary conditions of such a teaching situation. When we have had the chance to talk privately to these teachers over lunch or coffee the question has often been rephrased as, 'Yes, but do the units produce anything that I can mark/assess/show to parents/display on the notice board?'. This is a very fair question and I shall answer it as fully as possible.

First of all, it must be said that although growth of awareness is a major objective of *Language in Use* and awareness appears to be a concept that is hard to measure, there is nothing abstract about the way in which this objective is pursued. Pupils cannot be made aware of anything without something for them to work with and without using their abilities to perform particular tasks. Now very many of the tasks or activities which are suggested in the units produce an end product that is similar to the end product of more traditional ways of working. It may be a written report, an analysis of figures, a collection of cuttings or poems, a tape-recording of a discussion, a script for acting, an article for a newspaper, or an essay. There is such a very wide range of options open to the teacher in pursuing any unit that the kind of work produced by pupils can easily be shaped to fit the needs of the teaching situation without in any way limiting the scope of the teacher's work. If a weekly 'essay' *must* be produced, then there is no reason why it cannot arise from work with a unit or be a way of drawing together what has been done. Teachers may well find that the quality of this written work improves, because it arises out of a situation which has engaged the interest and enthusiasm of pupils. It has become more meaningful to them to write, because what they write is a necessary part of what they are doing. Indeed, many teachers have found that the problem is not so much the need

35

to put pressure on pupils to produce written work, but the need to prevent themselves becoming inundated with what is produced! In schools where the accent on written work is less strong, but where tangible 'work' must still be produced, it may well be possible for a teacher to display material collected or organised by his pupils in the course of working with a unit. Recently, a former pupil of mine, now in her first year of teaching, told me how she had been visited regularly by a Head teacher whose concern with the progress of her class of mixed 6-, 7- and 8-year-olds was expressed entirely in terms of how long a particular piece of their work had been on the notice board. In that school, the frequent changing of the notice board was a sign that good hard work was going on, while infrequent changing was a sign of 'slackness'. In such a situation, a teacher may well find that the units actually increase the flow of visible 'work'.

'But what about the quality of the work?' There is no short and simple answer to the question of what one means by 'quality' of work, but there are two important factors in the production of written work which bear upon the question. We can call them the 'time factor' and the 'content factor'. First, the time factor. Most of the readers of this book, and certainly both of the writers, were educated in a world where speed was equated with ability. Consider these common phrases: 'Never has to think twice about it, out it comes'; 'Bright little lad, always has an answer'; 'Very articulate man—no humming and haaing, he always has something to say'. All these phrases are phrases of approval and the reader will be equally familiar with their opposites. A pupil who pauses before answering is criticised for being slow, not praised for thinking through the possibilities of the question. Now when it comes to writing in school, the same situation is repeated, because it is very difficult for teachers to be patient. Having themselves been urged to 'Get a move on and not sit there all day thinking', and having successfully adjusted to the demands made upon them, they tend to fall into the habit of repeating the pattern with their own pupils who are struggling to work out, not only *what* they want to say, but *how* they are going to say it. Many teachers expect pupils to 'get it down', clearly and acceptably the first time of asking, and to express themselves in 'simple, logical English', without realising what an extraordinarily complex business this has been shown to be.

Let me illustrate this last point by taking the one situation adults encounter which is similar to the situation pupils meet when they are required to produce a piece of written work. Consider what happens when we find we have to write a letter to a company complaining about faulty goods or services, or a letter to our bank manager regarding a loan or overdraft, or a letter to the Income Tax objecting to a Notice of Coding, or a letter of condolence to a close friend. The readers of this book can certainly manage these tasks, but do they manage to sit down and write them straight off? Is there not a period during which the letter is 'in one's mind'? Phrases are tried out in the head. The task is put off, because one 'can't quite think what to say'. When we do sit down to write, is there not likely to be more than one attempt at 'getting the tone right'? It is possible to say that the examples I have chosen are 'difficult' and that any of us could write a letter to a friend 'without thinking', but the situation in which pupils work is seldom similar to the ease and informality of 'writing to a friend'. It is much more like the situation I have described where a monitoring of tone, content and style is critical to the acceptability of the finished letter.

Looked at from this point of view what a pupil produces in class, or for homework is, at best, a 'first draft'. Like our first attempt at a difficult letter, it may by no means represent what that pupil is capable of, but how often does he get a second chance to work on a piece of writing? How often does he get the chance to realise that the tone of his writing is too formal or too informal; that the content is not organised in the best possible way; that, as my geographers found out, they have not got all the material they need for what they are trying to do?

Many of the units do create opportunities for pupils to review and rewrite their work, and group discussion is used as a means to this end. Having to explain something to someone else clarifies one's own thoughts and this kind of clarification is possible for each individual pupil in the context of the small group. When they come to rewrite what they have done, the talk and discussion will have helped them to shape what they want to say. Consequently, the work produced will certainly be better than the pupil's first attempt, but *it will have taken time*, and it will have required a great deal of tolerance and patience on the part of the teacher in the initial stages of this process. One of the hardest things for a teacher to do is to stand back and watch a group apparently muddle backwards and forwards arguing about a word or a phrase. It would appear to be *so much quicker* just to tell them what they need, but when I tried telling my geographers how to write essays I got nowhere. Perhaps a part of what is being said here is best summed up for us by the comment of one teacher who used the units rather unwillingly, because his Head of Department thought they were a good idea. Initially, this teacher felt that too much time was spent letting pupils 'muddle around', instead of 'getting on with it'. However, he continued the work he had been asked to do and eventually wrote in his report:

> The thought has also been nagging me that perhaps we should do less teaching, let the children do more for themselves and observe whether in fact they consequently learn more or less.

Certainly the comments of many other teachers concerned with the quality of pupils' written work would support this teacher's insight.

In the last paragraph, I suggested that, if a pupil is to produce good written work, then a key factor is the time allowed him, time to develop his thinking and to review his first draft. This is assuming, however, that there *is* a first draft. For many teachers the problem is to get pupils to write anything at all. So we come to the question of the content factor. What can pupils write about? For many pupils, the request to write about 'Summer Holidays', or 'How I spend my Saturday', is really like an adult going to the Doctor because he is feeling dreadful, and being asked to give a full report of his condition. Where does he start? What is relevant? What does the Doctor really want to know? And as many of us know full well, what really troubles us or makes us anxious the doctor may dismiss without comment. The position for pupils faced with a blank sheet of paper and a request for writing is somewhat similar. Even when the topic does relate to their immediate interests, and not to what a colleague of ours has called, 'The adventures of that damned ubiquitous penny', it is still an almost impossible task for many pupils to organise their thinking, to decide what, if anything, about their summer holidays or their Saturday is interesting or describable. The units help by letting the writing arise in context, as part of doing a job, and because there is a job to do, there is a focus for selecting what is relevant, there is something that can be said. The pupil can concentrate on how to say what needs saying rather than on finding something to say for the sake of handing it in.

For example, on one occasion I had four groups of twelve-year-olds working out the problem of whether they would rather be the wife of a Cypriot peasant or the wife of a Californian wage labourer. We had studied the lives of both peasant and wage labourer and there was a great deal to discuss, for each way of life had its advantages and disadvantages. After lengthy discussion, one group called me over. 'We're stuck', said one girl. 'We have all these things here in Cyprus like being poor, but owning your own land and being independent. Here in California we have things like washing machines and big, big cars and power schemes, and there must be a word for this sort of thing to keep it different from things you feel.' There was indeed a word, there were several, and they worked out from what I offered that 'technology' was what they needed. What they did not have to worry about was finding something to say. They had a great deal to say, because they could make perfectly good sense of the problems of a wage labourer being unemployed in a time of recession and of the difficulties of living on a peasant farm with very limited facilities and primitive methods of cultivation, so they focused instead on the task of deciding which they would prefer and explaining why this was so. The work they produced was lengthy, well illustrated and of a very high standard.

# III Teacher, pupil and unit

## 10 Does using the units affect pupil/teacher relationships?

First of all we must be quite clear about what we mean by 'the relationship between teacher and pupil', because we have found in talking to teachers that two very different meanings can be given to this phrase. Both meanings are important and both are affected by the units.

I can best show how these two meanings of 'teacher/pupil relationship' differ by looking into three classrooms. In the first classroom, thirty pupils in neat school uniform are sitting in four rows of desks. On a raised dais at the front of the room a serious young man is demonstrating Pythagoras's Theorem. He explains slowly and precisely the stages of the proof and at each stage he asks, 'Are you quite clear about that?'. He does not expect, and does not receive, any reply. As the lesson proceeds, he questions individuals on the sequence of operations in the theorem, reprimanding two boys who confuse steps in the sequence. In the course of the lesson, only one boy asks a question and at the end of the lesson the boys file out in silence.

In the second classroom a science lesson is taking place. The Science mistress is middle-aged and talks rather quickly as she describes the apparatus set up on her bench. The blackboard is covered with diagrams and as the lesson proceeds four groups of girls take notes on how to carry out the distillation experiment which is already set up on their benches. At a later stage in the lesson the teacher comes down from her dais and visits each table in turn asking, 'How's it going?' or 'Everything all right?'. There is a low level of conversation and questions are asked frequently about the practical details of the experiment underway.

In the third classroom, a young history teacher is engaged in describing the French Revolution. His description is a lively one, accompanied by animated gestures. Both he and the class are amused when, during his account of the guillotine, his karate-like chop on a pile of exercise books sends the whole lot sliding to the floor. Questions and comments are exchanged freely. 'Have you ever seen a guillotine, sir? I saw one on telly, but they moved the camera when the chopper was coming down on the bloke's head—they always do cut the good bits.' The bell which ends the lesson interrupts a lively discussion as to whether or not it was fair to cut off the king's head.

These three classrooms are presenting three very different patterns of *social* relationship. The three teachers described demonstrate quite different attitudes to their pupils. Metaphorically speaking, the 'social distance' they establish between themselves and their pupils varies from several miles in the case of the young man teaching Pythagoras, to inches only in the case of the young historian. This idea of 'social distance' is well recognised in our common use of language. Consider the meaning of phrases like, 'He's a cold fish. Always keeps his distance'; 'A rum character that. Keeps himself to himself'; 'Always hobnobbing with his cronies in the office'; 'Not the type one wants to rub shoulders with'; 'Formal type, he is. Never yet heard him use a Christian name', and so on. 'Social distance', or the gap people maintain between each other when face to face in a shared social situation, is, therefore, the first of the two meanings teachers have in mind when they ask about the effect of the units upon their relationship with their pupils.

Teachers are very much aware that social distance is a crucial factor in the learning situation, and most staffrooms contain a range of divergent views on the subject of what is, and is not, an appropriate social distance to maintain between teacher and pupil. For example, were our three teachers to share a staffroom, one might find the mathematician and the historian in serious conflict. The mathematician feels that he is there to teach, not to entertain. He feels that detachment from his pupils is appropriate to the objectivity of the job in hand and that the historian is lowering the dignity of the profession by his antics, and, incidentally, making it much more difficult for him to maintain the distance *he* deems appropriate. On the other hand, the historian accuses the mathematician of being unsympathetic to his pupils and argues that unless they are allowed to come to terms with their teacher as a person they will never care about anything he teaches. He must meet them on their terms.

The Science mistress on the other hand has never viewed her job in terms of 'being familiar' or 'being distant'. She has always behaved in a way which she felt was suited to getting the job done, and for her this meant being approachable as far as the work itself was concerned. She considers the mathematician somewhat unapproachable, and feels that this is a disadvantage to his pupils, as they cannot present their difficulties freely, and she finds the behaviour of the historian disconcerting, although she admits that his way of behaving seems to be successful in interesting pupils who have previously shown little interest in anything at all.

Let me leave this question of the social distance between teacher and pupil for the moment and look at the other meaning which teachers give to the relationship between teacher and pupil. Once more, I shall use the three classrooms, but this time I want to look at the relationship between teachers and pupils in terms of *their relationship to knowledge*. In this case, there is no essential difference between the three classrooms: the teacher has the knowledge and the pupil has not. All the information introduced into the learning situation is provided by the teacher and all the activity going on is related to what the teacher himself has provided. The pupil's task is to assimilate what is provided. He is not expected to contribute any information, or to have any significant information to contribute, and, consequently, no part of the activity of the classroom stems from what he has contributed. Now there are many teachers today who would argue that, unless the pupil is allowed to make a real contribution to the learning situation, effective learning cannot take place. Consequently, when these teachers ask questions about the relationship between teacher and pupil the units require, they are thinking in terms of who contributes what to the learning situation. They want to know if there is any opportunity for the pupil to contribute his own information to the work; if any use is made of the pupil's own experience or observations; if it all has to come from the teacher.

The original question has now been restated in two different forms; does using the units affect the social distance between teachers and pupils and does using the units affect the traditional way of presenting knowledge? How, then, am I to answer? Let me begin by looking into a fourth classroom. The situation recorded here is one we observed when a colleague decided to use unit F4, 'National Characteristics', with a class of fifteen-year-old boys in a school in Belfast. Some days before this particular session took place a discussion had arisen about the appearance and manner of an English politician who had been seen on television. Many of the boys expressed the opinion that the English were 'cold' and our colleague decided to use F4, 'National Characteristics', in order to broaden the discussion and to prepare the way for a study he had planned of George Orwell's essay, 'Boys' Weeklies'.

The class arrived in groups and went to the notice boards to look at some sketches which had just been put up. Some boys returned books to the class library. The teacher handed some duplicated material to a small group and asked them to spread it round.

Pupil 1: 'What's this, sir?'
Teacher: 'What does it look like?'

42

Pupil 2: 'I dunno, a quiz?'
Pupil 3: 'What do we have to do with it?'
Teacher: 'Is everyone here?'

By the time the teacher asked this question most of the boys were already studying the duplicated sheet which had, a list of nationalities along the top which included Americans, Arabs, Australians, French, and a list of characteristics such as 'clever', 'cold', 'cowardly', 'dependable', 'dirty', along the side. Some boys were arguing as to whether Americans were clever. At this point, the teacher reminded the class of their discussion about the coldness of Englishmen and said that he wondered if there were other characteristics commonly associated with other nationalities. He suggested the boys work in groups of four or five, and that one boy act as recorder for each group, putting a tick in the appropriate box when the group agreed to assign a particular characteristic to a particular nationality.

Tables were moved round, there was a buzz of talk and then the questions began.

Pupil 1: 'Sir, do you put what you think yourself, or what you think people think?'
Teacher: 'Let each group decide that themselves.'
Pupil 2: 'Sir, if there's a characteristic that isn't there, what do you do?'
Teacher: 'What were you thinking of?'
Pupil 3: 'Well, we think Italians and French are very arty, but that's not on, is it?'
Teacher: 'Fair enough, why don't you add it on the side? Is there anything else anyone wants to add?'

Four more items were added. They were 'idealistic', 'reserved', 'generous' and 'determined'.

Pupil 4: 'Sir, it's all foreigners. What about Ulstermen?'
Teacher: 'Well, what about them?'
Pupil 4: 'Well, can't we put them on, on the top?'
Teacher: 'Right, anyone else you want to add?'
Pupils: 'No, there's no more room.'

The teacher circulates. He is called on by various groups. Two groups with even numbers have a problem, because they have split two and two over a number of decisions. With his help they agree to put crosses on the sheet where disagreement has occurred. After about twenty minutes, the teacher asks for the attention of the class.

He has drawn a grid on the board identical with the grid on the sheets which the boys have been marking. He now asks the group reporter to put up a hand when he calls out a category which the group have ticked.

A pattern begins to emerge. The characteristics of some national groups have been completely agreed on: Americans are 'clever', 'hard-working', 'kind', 'well dressed', and 'generous'. Italians are 'excitable', 'funny', 'kind', 'lazy' and 'artistic'. With other groups, however, there is much argument. The class thinks that Ulstermen are thought of as 'dirty', 'drunken', 'excitable' and 'funny', but that this is only true of some Ulstermen and that representations of Ulstermen on television are not entirely fair. This leads to the question of how one forms opinions of people one does not know. The teacher asks if any members of the class know any individuals of the nationalities listed and whether or not they fit the pattern on the board.

Towards the end of the session, the idea of a stereotype develops from talk about 'Stage Irishmen', and the teacher asks for other examples of stereotypes. Cowboy 'baddies' and German officers are mentioned and one boy points out that his father's view of Germans is quite different from his own view. This leads to the suggestion from another boy that they should take their duplicated sheets home and try them out on parents. Extra sheets are distributed and the session ends with the class comparing what their fathers think.

Now it will be easy for the reader to see that our teacher with the Pythagorean theorem would be very unhappy in this situation. For him, there would be two main problems: firstly, the social distance between teacher and pupil would be much too close for his liking; and secondly, a great deal of the information content of the session is being provided by the pupils from their own experience. This produces a situation which is more informal and more flexible, more 'messy' than he could easily tolerate. Our historian, however, would be pleased at the narrowing of social distance, though one suspects that he might have difficulty in subordinating his own exuberance to the dominant role played by pupils. There is also the question of how he would react to the fact that the pupils were contributing a great deal to the content of the lesson. The situation I have described does not give him much opportunity to exploit his taste for dramatic monologue. Rather, it requires him, in this session at least, to adopt what we may now call 'a low profile' in order that his pupils can make the maximum possible contribution to the work themselves. In principle, he may say he would be pleased at the increased oppor-

44

tunity which pupils have for bringing their own experience into the classroom, but ultimately he may not want to move towards this way of teaching any more than his mathematician colleague, because he is as intent on teaching 'history' as the other is intent on teaching 'geometry'.

Using the units does indeed affect the relationship between teacher and pupil in both senses of the phrase. It changes the social distance between them and it changes the balance between the contributions which each of them makes to the learning situation. Why it should be necessary for the units to use ways of working that lead to such changes is a question in itself, which I take up in Section 13, p. 54. For the moment, however, let us stay in the classroom and consider what problems there might be for both teacher and pupil in learning situations such as the one we have just considered.

## 11 What does this mean for teachers?

What I want to do in this section is to focus attention on the teacher himself and look at the learning situation which the units create entirely through his eyes. How will a teacher feel? What will be new? What might make him anxious? How can the units themselves help him to adjust to the new situation they themselves create, given that he has decided to go ahead and use them?

In Section 3, 'Working through a unit', I described one of my own bad moments when working with my first unit. What I said was this:

Three things occurred to me at that point. Firstly, how my Head-mistress would react, if, drawn by the laughter she appeared and found the prospective A-level candidates studying the *Daily Mirror*. Secondly, how she would react to the sight of a normally active member of staff standing by the window apparently doing nothing; and thirdly, how I myself was going to react if I found that, at the end of whatever period of time I chose to spend on this activity, I had not in fact achieved anything. . . .

It seems to me now, looking back on that situation, that these three questions all related to one thing, the fact that I was aware something had changed in my relationship with my pupils, but that I could not immediately see what it was. It was not a question of social distance, for I had always chosen to work *with* my pupils, yet something was making me uneasy. At the time, I would have said that it was my 'doing nothing' or the fact that I found myself feeling superfluous. Having talked to many other teachers since that day, who have had a similar experience to mine, I now can see the problem more clearly

45

for what it was, and it seems to me that what was causing the anxiety was a certain change in my role as a teacher, a change which the units had brought about and which I could not quite define for myself. It was not that I had really been rendered superfluous by the units, but I was being asked to work in a way to which I was not accustomed. Instead of being the sole provider of information, mostly through direct verbal contact, I was being asked to organise resources for my pupils so that they could use the information themselves and, at the same time, make their own contribution to it. I was also being asked to act as a consultant, to help with problems, suggest further lines of exploration and redirect the work when it ran into difficulties. What I was really being asked to do was to set aside the formal presentation of information for much of the time and to provide what information was needed by becoming an organiser and consultant instead. The description of the work with the unit on 'National Characteristics' in the previous section is an excellent demonstration of all these points.

Initially, some teachers find that it is difficult to adjust to this change. They cannot always see that being an organiser and consultant is indeed 'doing something' just as much as presenting information formally; or that they are using their skill and judgment just as much in selecting resources and directing the course of the work as they did when they selected the content of what they presented. Even when the teacher does accept, however, that he is 'doing something' a further problem may arise, for the new situation which using the units creates is not as predictable as the old, and the flexibility of the work may mean that the teacher is asked for information by his pupils which he does not have available. For a teacher who prides himself on knowing his stuff, this can be very disconcerting. Perhaps I can best illustrate this by recounting a story told to me very ruefully by a Yorkshire teacher. This teacher had decided to try unit B4, 'Notices', with his class of sixteen-year-old boys and girls. The class went out to discover what notices they could find in the vicinity of the school and local streets and to note how they were used. When they returned, the teacher 'wished that he had never heard of *Language in Use*'. The reason was that one boy had produced from the local Post Office the notice, 'Docs Ernie know where you live?'. The teacher embarked upon an explanation of 'Ernie' and could not get beyond 'Random Number Indicator' when it came to spelling out the initials E.R.N.I.E. In the end, the class said that they would find out for him on their way home from school. This piece of work eventually led on to the unit on 'New words' and the teacher decided, firstly, that it was reasonable not to know *everything* and that, secondly, he rather enjoyed the enthusiasm his class had shown when they were offered the opportunity of going and finding out something which he had not been able to supply for them! However happily this particular story ended, it does demonstrate nevertheless that there was indeed an adjustment to be made. This teacher had to come to terms with the idea of a teacher in his own classroom 'not knowing everything'. For so many teachers, educated in the tradition of the subject specialist and teaching as subject specialists themselves, this is often the major adjustment to be made in the course of learning how to use the units.

Adjusting to a change in social distance, however, can be just as much of a problem. There are two ways in which this can come about. First, the teacher himself may be uneasy about the less formal relationships which arise from using the units, like the very honest teacher, mentioned in Section 7, who told me that he could accept my argument for working this way, but felt that he himself could not cope. On the other hand, the teacher himself may be easy about these less formal relationships, but may be anxious, as indeed I was, about the attitude of his Headmaster or his colleagues, particularly those who feel that no 'real work' can be done by pupils who are not working in silence at individual desks. There is no complete answer to this problem, but one part of the answer lies in the teacher's ability to answer the questions, 'What are you doing?', and 'Why are you doing it?'. One of the main objectives of this book is to put any teacher using *Language in Use* in the position where he can show a questioner what it is doing and explain why the units need to work in the particular way that they do. By the end of the book, I hope to have provided the reader with a body of information about the units, about teaching and learning, and about learning and using language, which will answer to his needs when he is challenged to defend the work he is doing with *Language in Use*.

Unlike the young lecturer in Section 1 who got so enthusiastic about *Language in Use* that he thought he had made it sound like 'Snibbo', the miracle cure for all ills, I think that, in my attempt to show where the problems may lie, I may have given the impression that it is all too difficult. It may look as if I am saying that the units make a demand upon the teacher that requires a total change of outlook and technique. This is certainly not the case. Firstly, it is highly unlikely that any one teacher will encounter *all* the problems I have listed here; and secondly, there is no suggestion that any teacher will want to use units, and only units, as a basis for his work. *Language in Use* is not being offered as an alternative to all other ways of teaching, but as an additional resource, designed to meet the teacher's need for a guide to work with language, whatever his teaching situation.

There is no 'right way' of using the units. A teacher can move at his own pace in using them. He can use the same unit many times with different classes so that he becomes familiar with the kinds of response it gives rise to; or he can move out from a unit into other ways of working and back again, so that he has time to think through what he has observed. What this means for many teachers is that the units have provided not only a resource for the day-to-day planning of lessons but a stimulus to their own thinking, and a support by means of which they have been able to review their own practice as teachers and to gain a much greater insight into the needs of pupils, both linguistic and educational.

## 12 What does this mean for pupils?

Just as a teacher may have difficulty in adjusting to the new situation created by using the units, so indeed may the pupil, for he may well have acquired a set of attitudes and assumptions about school and learning which make it extremely difficult for him to participate in the kind of learning situation the units create.

The heart of the problem lies in that last phrase 'participate in the learning situation', because the units ask the pupil to become a participant just as they ask the teacher to become an organiser and consultant. He no longer has the option of sitting behind his desk, a passive recipient, knowing that if he looks intent all will be well. Instead, he is asked to discuss, to report, to research, to play an active part in his own learning, and to go out of school and bring back the results of his observations. Furthermore, he is asked to do all this in collaboration with other pupils in the class. It is not surprising that his reaction may sometimes be a rather hurt, 'Who *me*?' or a belligerent, 'Not on your life'. He is puzzled at being put in the position where he has to make up his own mind what to do instead of being told what to do and how to do it.

One of the first problems for the pupil is a social one. Not the immediately obvious matter of the less formal relationship with his teacher, but the much more complicated question of his relationship with his peers. No matter how well he may get on with other members of his class, inside or outside school, learning how to *work* with them is likely to be a new experience for him. Moreover, behind the pupil, there lies the customary habits of his community. In some communities individuals come to feel that what they think, what opinions they have, are so intimately a part of themselves that if someone

48

disagrees with their opinion, then, the disagreement must be *personal*. The situation is summed up very sharply by Jeremy Seabrook in his book, *The Unprivileged*. There he says that the people he knew in the Northampton working-class community in which he grew up:

> . . . were not capable of abstract argument. Every opinion expressed was regarded as a fundamental characteristic of the person expressing it, a physical attribute like the colour of his hair or the shape of his nose (and perhaps in this they were not entirely wrong) and an attack upon the opinions was the equivalent of a personal bodily assault, and the transition to physical force was a quick and logical process.

Pupils from such communities bring into the classroom with them the attitudes of their own community and the ways of using language for expressing differences of view which they have learnt with them. The teacher may well be unaware of these attitudes, but they may be crucial in their effect upon his work. Let me give an example. Towards the end of my last year of teaching in Belfast, I began to apply some of the insights I had derived from my early work with the units to a mixed ability group of twelve-year-olds. On this particular occasion, they were working in small groups. Their task was to select from a group of annotated diagrams which they had produced at home the one which would best demonstrate the concept of chemical weathering to a member of the class who was absent. The groups were considering all aspects of the diagram, its information content, its presentation, the quality of the descriptive notes and indeed the accuracy of the spelling. Talking to one group who had called me over to help them I was startled by an outburst of anger from the group immediately behind me. I turned round to find two girls glaring at each other in fury. As I moved towards them in the silence which had suddenly fallen, one of the two appealed to me, 'Miss, she says this is chemical weathering and I say it's air pollution, look (she pulled at my sleeve) that smoke there's going into the air and polluting it'. The rest of the group were quite taken aback at the violence of the outburst. I looked at the diagram. A red factory was belching out black smoke which rose into the sky forming a cloud. From the cloud, grey rain dropped on to a white house with grey patches on its walls and a row of drooping flowers in its front garden.

'Well, actually, you are both right', I said. 'You've got a very good idea here.' I then tried to explain that what you called it depended on the way you looked at it and the problem you were trying to solve. Smiles appeared and rather nervous laughter when another member of the group said, 'Miss, I thought they were going to have a fight'. For me, there were two very important features in this particular incident. The first was, of course, the degree of violence which disagreement had led to. In one way it was no surprise to me. How could it be in a city already involved in the violence engendered by the assumption that 'There's only one way of seeing things and that's ours'? I had not seen it so clearly revealed in the learning situation, however. I had not before considered that attitudes to 'right and wrong' might be a factor in a pupil's ability to handle concepts like chemical weathering or air pollution. What using this particular way of working had done was to alert me to difficulties which the pupils were experiencing, difficulties the origins of which lay quite outside the orbit of school itself. I can think of few other ways in which this important piece of information about these pupils could have come to me.

Secondly, this incident shows how successfully pupils can cope with a taxing situation when it occurs in the course of work which has interested and excited them, and when they are allowed the time to think things through at their own pace and, initially, *in language of their own choosing*. What the reader cannot know from my account of this incident is that the girl who appealed to me so passionately was a girl who had never before spoken in class, though I had been doing my best to help and encourage her for eighteen months, a girl who was reported to be 'of a very low IQ' and who 'shouldn't really be at a school like this'. Over the period of months in which I had been using ways of working adapted from the units, she had gained confidence through her participation in the talk of the group, she had grown used to the idea that she could formulate an opinion and state it successfully, so that when she was faced with the problem of whether she was 'right' or 'wrong' over this question of pollution, an issue of burning importance to her, she was ready and able to enlist my support. From this point on, she lost all her former 'shyness' and, by the time the year ended, her enthusiasm for a subject in which she appeared to 'know' something enabled her at last to put down on paper successfully what she now felt confident of saying.

One could continue to illustrate at length the new ways of speaking that a pupil is encouraged to learn as a result of working with the units but many of these ways of speaking are better discussed more fully in the next chapter. What should be said here is that it is by no means only the units of *Language in Use* that are now making this sort of demand on pupils' ways of speaking in the learning situation. A scientist colleague has told us of the problems which many teachers encountered in the early days of the Nuffield Science Project. Pupils and teachers met face-to-face over new apparatus, and new techniques for scientific explorations, and did not know what to say to each other. Unlike the science lesson described in Section 10, all the information was not to pass down from teacher to pupil; it was to arise from a joint effort of enquiry. The problems arose because a joint effort of this kind was an entirely new experience for both teachers and pupils, and involved an alteration in the social distance between them, as well as a change in their relationship to the content of the lesson. Finding the relevant new ways of speaking was as taxing as anything arising out of the enquiry itself, for both teachers and pupils.

While *Language in Use* deliberately sets out to create situations in which pupils are encouraged to extend their use of language by drawing upon the knowledge they have already, and consequently offers a proper support and guidance for this activity, materials like the Nuffield Science courses, the Humanities Curriculum Project, or *Lifeline*, the materials developed by the Moral Education Project, make similar demands without always being aware of the fact. Critically, the ways of working required by these materials put a very heavy demand upon pupils' ability to use spoken language for expressing a personal point of view; for reasoning; for entering into discourse that is concerned with planning and decision making; for qualifying, or even rejecting, their own view previously stated; for questioning the views of others and for offering their own qualifications of those views. All these activities put a very considerable strain upon the linguistic competence of the pupil who is not accustomed to such ways of speaking as a normal feature of his experience of language, in school or outside it. In particular, implicit in their use is the speaker's ability to tolerate their use by others and this requires of him a subordination to the progress of the talk, a willingness to suspend his own contribution, or modify it in the light of what others say before he speaks, that amounts to the learning of a very sophisticated pattern of social behaviour. Such a pattern is not necessarily easily or rapidly learnt, especially by those to whom it is entirely unfamiliar. It is not surprising, therefore, that pupils who have done work with the units seem to be much more at home with the work generated by these materials than those who have not. It is not that they 'know more' about Science, Humanities or Moral Education, but that they have been able to develop some of the social skills which collaboration and consultation require.

Certainly, work with the units is not a soft option. For many pupils it is as challenging as anything else they could be offered. What the field trials showed, however, time after time, was the way in which they were able to meet this challenge, and respond vigorously to it, if they were given the right resources, the time, and, at critical points, the encouragement they needed. On the other hand, it is fair to say that, if things did get too difficult for pupils, they had a variety of ways of shifting the pressure. One course of action, which we discussed in Section 7, was to revert to silence. For some groups of pupils, however, action meant trying to get things back to normal: 'Sir, this isn't English/Geography/History. The last teacher read us poems/ showed us slides/ gave us notes' is often the sign that a class want to get back behind the comforting barricade of a desk and leave it all to sir.

This was the approach a class of sixteen-year-olds at a Nottingham Comprehensive school adopted. Their teacher had decided to try unit B5, 'Front Page', which is concerned with the way in which the expressive content of a message can be modified by the way it is presented. The aim of the unit 'is to show how the overall pattern of the front page of a newspaper provides a context which can influence how we interpret the message of any single item in it'. The unit did not go well. Although the boys and girls knew each other well, they had not worked together before. Initially, 'discussion' took the form of one person presenting an opinion and another person telling them they were wrong. There was a good deal of unproductive bickering. Soon the class was asking, 'Sir, what are we supposed to be doing?'. The teacher was most unhappy about the whole activity, for, although this was a 'difficult' class, containing some particularly aggressive individuals, he found their behaviour in the small group situation worse than in the whole-class situation, where they were normally fairly willing to do what was asked of them. The teacher persevered, we are told, only because of an impending visit from a member of the *Language in Use* team and the school's commitment to participation in the field trials. After the fourth session the teacher had made a long list of criticisms which he hoped would be of value to his forthcoming visitor and he decided that the fifth session, visitor or no visitor, would be the last. This fifth session was to be devoted to making a front page because the work had progressed so slowly. The class arrived. To the teacher's surprise they had all remembered to bring the necessary newspapers which they had been asked to collect over the weekend. Before he had quite collected himself, the teacher noticed that scissors and paste were disappearing from the box on his desk and that bags and books were being put on windowsills to leave the table surfaces quite clear for the trial layouts which were being pieced together like jigsaws. The teacher had not as yet said anything. There was a buzz of conversation. The teacher abandoned his planned opening remarks and substituted a general 'Everybody all right, then?', which elicited some replies of 'Yes' and a number of requests for large sheets of paper, more paste and Sellotape. Something had happened. After four sessions which had been highly uncomfortable for the teacher, and apparently not at all productive for the pupils, there was now a working atmosphere which was all that he could wish for. He was puzzled. He leant back against the wall and surveyed the room, looking for an explanation. Was it something in the weekend's newspapers that had caught their interest? Were they making a special effort in order to humour him? At this critical point, a boy, usually considered 'tough', looked up momentarily from his cutting, saw the teacher's thoughtful and puzzled look, and said:

Why don't you nip off to the Staffroom for a cuppa, sir? I'll come and getya if we need anything.

We have always regretted that the teacher's response at that precise moment was not recorded, but the incident does illustrate the hard fact that there is likely to be a 'period of confusion' during which it is exceedingly difficult for the teacher to make an accurate assessment of what is really going on. This 'period of confusion', however, is vital to the effective learning of new patterns of social behaviour such as I have discussed in this section. Moreover, other things *were* going on. Under the cloak of the confusion, the key decisions were being made, so that, when the groups came to put together their front pages, they knew just what they wanted to do. Finally, it must be said that this extreme form of the 'period of confusion' usually has to be gone through once only with any one group. Just as my geographers went on using the new concept of audience they had gained whenever they had writing to do, so this class were able to use their new-found skills for working together, for using talk to state views, make decisions and solve problems, independently of the context of the units. This also suggests that there is considerable value in planning to use several units over a period of time, for one is then able to capitalise on the time and energy the pupils have put into their first experience of learning how to work with the units.

# IV Pupils' use of spoken and written English

## 13 Why do the units use these ways of working?

The ways of working used in the units are, as I have said before, by no means new or unfamiliar. They are ways of working which some teachers have used for a very long time. What is relevant at this point of the discussion, however, is that they use these ways of working much more systematically and frequently than most teachers might normally decide to do. The fact that work in small groups, talk and discussion, pupils making their own decisions about what to do, teachers acting as consultants, pupils rather than teachers presenting the results of their work to the whole class, play so large a part in the design of the units is not fortuitous, and is certainly not dictated by any current vogue for these things. The purpose of this section, therefore, is to show that the activities the units recommend arise out of a coherent and explicit view of the part language plays in our lives. What the units ask pupils to do is the practical classroom realisation of what we know about the way in which human beings learn and use language as an inescapable part of the business of living.

Once more, let me begin by looking at what is going on in one particular classroom. On this occasion, the class was a group of 'B-stream' girls in a small grammar school in Belfast. A fair proportion of these girls had not passed the 11+ examination. The Science teacher had had great difficulty in getting the girls to write up their experiments, so she had worked out a version of Unit A3, 'Judging your audience', to try to meet the situation. It was February and ten of her thirty pupils had been absent. When they returned she set up the following pattern of work. The girls were grouped in threes and in each group there was one girl who had been absent. To this girl, the teacher gave the notebook of a girl who had written a report of an experiment done while she had been away. The girl who had been absent then tried to carry out the experiment for herself and her group, using only the information in the notebook which she had been given. The two members of her group were not allowed to help actively but they were asked to observe carefully and to record any difficulties which might occur. The situation had its lighter moments, particularly when one girl read out the instruction, 'Hold the test tube vertically in the flame', and expressed fairly forcibly her reluctance to carry out the instruction without a pair of tongs! When all the experiments had been attempted, the groups then settled down to see if any difficulties had occurred. In most cases, the report on the experiment had not been specific about measurements, e.g., 'Put the crystals', rather than 'Put 2 grammes of crystals'; they had not been explicit enough about the actual sequence of events necessary for the experiment, or what operations needed to be carried out. The groups listed their comments and criticisms of the original report they had to use for the experiment and then went on to produce a new version of the report. These new versions were then redistributed amongst the groups and the experiment was done again to test out how successfully the comments on the original reports had been incorporated into the new ones. Finally, the whole class discussed the results of the changes and worked out a set of basic rules for setting down the sequence of operations involved in an experiment.

The situation which I have described above was another use of a unit, which had already been used quite differently in other contexts, as I have described in Sections 3 and 4 and Section 8, page 34. In this section, I want to show how this unit fulfils the key objectives which it shares with *all* the units, that is, the development of pupils' awareness and their command of language. I shall also show how these two objectives relate to the overall aim of the units, which is to develop a pupil's ability to use his language effectively, spoken or written, whatever and wherever the context might be.

How then is it possible to make a pupil aware that the report of a scientific experiment needs to be written in a particular way if it is to be an accurate record of the sequence of operations involved; that the characteristics we attribute to members of different nationalities derive from unexamined stereotypes we pick up from the culture of our own communities; or that the way the front page of a newspaper is organised can affect our assessment of the information it is conveying? All the evidence we have, either from our knowledge of how we actually use language in our everyday lives or, more particularly, from the field trials of *Language in Use*, suggests that awareness cannot come from telling pupils what is the case. If pupils do not become aware of such matters merely through being told about them, what can one do? The answer the units suggest is that one has to create situations in which pupils are free to use their own knowledge of how language is used and their own powers of observation in order to work out for themselves what might be the case. For example, the girl who attempts to carry out a scientific experiment using a classmate's notebook sees that she cannot manage, because she has not been given the right information in the right order. She has become aware of the limitations of a report that is unordered, and the fact that order and sequence are not a whim of the teacher, but a necessary adjustment to the job. She has become aware of a necessity in the use of language that does not derive from the arbitrary rules of school, but from the nature of logical thought itself.

I am sure the reader can recall similar examples of the development of awareness from the other classroom situations I have used. What all the examples have in common is the fact that the awareness concerned arose out of a situation where the pupil was helped to focus, not on what he did not know, but on what he did know and had not had the opportunity to make explicit to himself or anyone else. The boys who worked on 'National Characteristics' (p. 42), knew a great deal about the popular attitudes in their community towards people of other nationalities, but what the unit did was to get them to focus upon the fact and this enabled them to go further and comment on the truthfulness or falseness of these attitudes, tested against their own observations.

Valuable as this awareness may appear to a reader, however, he may still ask, 'But how does this relate to a pupil's effective use of language?'. A major part of the answer to this question is that there is more to using language than finding words for what one wants to say. The first thing a speaker has to do in any situation is to find out what he wants these words for and what sort of words would fit the situation as he reads it. There are some similarities here to the position of the gasman who came the other day to look at my ill-functioning cooker, without either tools or spare parts. I was rather puzzled as to why he had come to do a job apparently so ill-equipped. When I asked him why he did not carry any tools or spares in his van he explained that that would be impossible. There were, he said, several hundred makes of cooker, and a range of tools suited to each major make of cooker, so that the possibility of his actually having in his van exactly what any one cooker needed was highly unlikely. It was more efficient to assess the job, work out what tools and spares were needed, and then come back again fully equipped. Now, a pupil may have an extensive repertoire of words and structures, and ways of using them, but, like the gasman, he cannot mobilise his resources until he knows what job he is to do. The girls doing the experiment had to imagine, first of all, what an operationally effective report would look like and using a report that was *not* adequate was an important part of this process. Their own observation helped them to develop their picture of what was needed and it was this mental picture of what was needed that was critical to the next stage of their thinking and writing.

This last statement is relevant, not only to the girls who are engaged in producing a scientific report, but to every human being in every situation in which he is called on to speak or to write. Before one can speak or write effectively, one must form an accurate idea of what form of words would make sense in that particular situation. Without this idea, a speaker finds himself in that common situation where he might say, 'Words failed me', or 'I couldn't think what to say', or 'I knew afterwards what I should have said'. The ways of working used in the units are designed to foster in pupils an awareness of what effective linguistic action might look like over a very wide range of situations so that words do not fail them. Awareness, however, is only one side of the process. How does the pupil learn to select effectively from the resources he has available to him now that he 'knows what he wants to say'? Without the appropriate awareness of the linguistic demands of the situation anything he says is likely to be sadly inadequate to his needs at that moment. Awareness of itself, however, is not sufficient to carry him through. What will help the pupil to find the language for what he now knows he wants to say?

Consider once more the situation as it was at the end of the first stage of the work the girls did on writing up experiments. In one group, a girl managed to complete the experiment, but the notes she was working from were only a shaky guide, and she had to guess at the missing information, helped by her prior knowledge of the subject. Her two friends had made notes about her difficulties and then all three discuss what has been done. In that talk, they try to work out what the report should have said. They use what words they have and they try them out against the idea they have formed of what an effective report would be like. They have to go on to write the report, hence they are now required to put words on the page which will match the model report their discussion has outlined for them. This is a very different activity from a request to 'Write about your holidays', or 'Write about anything you like'. As we have seen, the girls carried out the task very satisfactorily and with little real difficulty. This sequence of work demonstrates how the units are able to develop pupils' command of language through the activities they recommend. It is at this point that I have to make a very obvious point, implicit in all that I have said so far in this section. We learn to use language, and we develop our command of language, *by using it*, just as we become fluent car-drivers by driving cars or skilful tennis players by playing tennis. The units aim to create conditions in which pupils learn to use language, and to develop their command of language, by using it. For example, the writing of the scientific report was preceded by talk and note-making: both of these activities enabled the pupils to rehearse what they needed to say before they tried to put the full version on paper. In the more flexible medium of speech they were able to try out alternatives and discover confusions and ambiguities in what they were saying.

The more talking and writing a pupil does, the more fluent he becomes at these activities; and the more fluent he becomes at speaking and writing the greater his awareness of the ways in which he can use language for speaking and writing. Awareness and command of language, therefore, must not be seen as consecutive steps in a process, in the way it has been convenient to represent them, but rather as two aspects of the same process, intimately interrelated to each other, so that any increase of the one involves a corresponding adjustment in the other. Hence any effective increase in pupils' awareness will contribute to developing their command of language and any increase in their command of language will equally contribute to the development of their awareness. Developed together as interrelating features of a single process by the ways of working which the units use they form the basis of that true growth in the pupils' overall ability to use language for living and for learning which so many teachers look for and hope to achieve.

## 14 'Talk' and 'discussion'

I have said a good deal already about 'talk' and 'discussion' in the process of talking about actual classroom situations and explaining why talk and discussion are used so systematically in the units, but so far I have not considered in detail the questions teachers ask about them. This section therefore takes a look at some of the basic characteristics of talk and discussion and how these relate to the anxieties teachers experience about talk in the classroom.

Let me begin with 'talk'. This is one of those occasions when I feel that a new word is needed, because the existing one is open to such a wide range of interpretation. Consider, for example, the expression 'Talking in class'. For most teachers the common meaning of the phrase is pejorative. It indicates a crime, major or minor, according to the teaching situation concerned. Such a view of 'talk' is not very encouraging when one wishes to present reasons for using talk as the most practical means for developing pupils' capacity to use language effectively. Setting that difficulty aside, however, there is also the fact that our common culture takes an equally unhelpful view of

58

'talk' and the part it plays in our lives. Consider what is implied by the meaning of the words and phrases we habitually use to refer to 'talk' in everyday life: 'Mere talk'; 'What we want is action, not words'; 'Talking gets you nowhere'; 'There's no use talking about it'; and, overheard in one College of Education staffroom, 'Well, there's no use sitting here talking about what we teach. Our job is to get on and put it over.'

All these common language phrases place a very low value on the usefulness of talk, and they completely fail to recognise in talk a mode of action. This is really very surprising, when we consider that human beings spend such a large part of their lives talking to each other; and that the very existence of their societies rests upon their ability to do so effectively. However, that is a matter for a different book, *Language and Community* (see Postscript, page 114). What I want to show in this section is the effect such a view of talk can have upon the attitudes of both teacher and pupil to its use in the classroom.

I would suggest that this effect is twofold. First the teacher may be profoundly uneasy about using talk as the units ask him to do, just because this view permeates the thinking of colleagues and parents. Especially in the initial stages, as we have seen, during the 'period of confusion', talk within a group is liable to be a fairly 'messy' activity. Listening in to what is said a teacher may become acutely aware that his pupils are not 'speaking in sentences'. For many teachers, listening to pupils talking in this way is an entirely novel experience. They have little by which to judge what they hear, because we do not normally 'listen in' to everyday conversation in this way. Most people assume that they do 'speak in sentences', because their model for what they *say* is not what they hear others say, but what they themselves *read*. The patterns of the written language shape their view of what all language patterns should be like and teachers are very little different from the majority of other people in this.

A teacher may also discover that pupils' talk is 'not logical', or rather, that the logic of the talk is different from what one imagines it should be. Some teachers argue that tape-recordings of pupils talking 'prove' that they do not speak in sentences, and that they do not stick to the point, so that one thing does not appear to lead to another. These teachers feel that pupils, as a whole, are not capable of 'productive' talk and that, consequently, the units should not be used with them. This is an unfortunate conclusion because it overlooks the fact that talk of any kind is likely to show similar characteristics. This apparent lack of 'grammatical' or 'logical' form is

59

exactly what constitutes the most noticeable difference between talk and writing. We do not normally speak in sentences, one at a time, each one following upon the other along a single line of argument, although there are times when we come very close to doing this if we have had a long experience of formal education, and have always had a great deal to do with books. It is for this reason that teachers in particular do indeed frequently use a form of spoken discourse which is virtually identical with the patterns of the written language. Perhaps it is by no means the least of our pupils' problems that their teachers so often talk like a book rather than a human being, in the sense that spoken discourse of this kind is very unusual in the ordinary course of living and does impose a very considerable burden upon the listener. Let the reader think of the last time he heard a celebrated University Professor in full flight, especially a time when the topic of the lecture was not entirely familiar to him. This will give him some idea of the strain a teacher's spoken discourse in the form of the written language can impose upon a pupil.

I must now take up the question of how, therefore, teachers can best come to terms with 'talk' in the classroom. Teachers have told us that they found two things especially helpful. Firstly, there is the study of 'talk' itself. One teacher tape-recorded part of a staff meeting, where the question of the wearing of uniform was being discussed; then part of a family discussion over the washing up after Sunday tea; and then part of a conversation between a group of pupils about a book which they had all read. After playing through the three tape-recordings at a local Teachers' Centre, she and her colleagues set out to produce written transcripts of the tapes. It was in the process of this activity that they came to see that one *can* study talk, and that talk in practice was very different from what they had imagined it to be. Secondly, teachers have pointed out the value of books which deal directly with the nature and function of talk and how talk relates to written language, such as *The Foundations of Language* and *Exploring Language*; and books which provide transcripts of real conversations with a commentary on them, such as *Language, the learner and the school* and *The Language of Primary School Children*. They have stressed the fact that, once they had found out about the true nature and function of talk and, especially, what their own spoken discourse looked like when it was transcribed, they rapidly developed a very different attitude to their pupils' talk and their use of talk. (See Books referred to in the text, page 118.)

Perhaps subject specialist teachers in particular need to know what talk is really like, because the only kind of talk so many of them have

60

come to value is the kind that they themselves experienced in studying their chosen subject, whether at school or college. Now this is the
kind of talk that we commonly single out and call 'discussion'.
Relatively, it is a very difficult form of talk for those unfamiliar with
it and it is seldom that pupils are really able to use it much before the
later years of school. Even then, they will only be able to enter into
discussion successfully if they have been given plenty of opportunity
to work out for themselves the control over free and personal self-
expression, over the content of what one says and the logic of its
presentation and over one's response to what others say, that this
form of talk demands. It is so often 'discussion', however, that
teachers adopt as their model for what 'talk' in the classroom ought
to look like. This leads them to judge that their 'average' pupils are
not capable of it; and that, consequently, they cannot benefit from
the units, because the units appear to make so much use of 'discussion'. The same argument has also been applied to other new
approaches, especially that offered by the Humanities Curriculum
Project. This view is surely the equivalent of saying that unless a
young rider is up to 'The Horse of the Year Show' he should not be
allowed to ride a horse; or that a five-year-old who does not understand his teacher's request to describe his house has thereby
demonstrated that he has no language!

Had I available an accepted set of terms to replace the single word
'talk', it would help me to show how very varied are the ways in
which human beings use this primary function of language. Such a
set of terms would help to distinguish more clearly between the
forms of talk we use primarily for relating ourselves to others and for
recounting our own experience, and the forms we use when we feel
the need to present an argument, or question the assumptions another
has made in an argument he has presented to us. Unfortunately, such
a set of terms does not yet exist. I hope, however, that I have said
enough to show that where we use the word 'talk' we are referring
to a wide range of *activities* that embrace great differences of form
and function. I would suggest that a reader now looks again at the
accounts of work done with the units that I gave in Sections 3 and
4, pages 10–18, Section 10, pages 42–43, Section 12, page 49, and
Section 13, page 54, and reconsider them in the light of what has
been said in this section. He should ask himself what opportunities
for talk are being created and of what kinds, and in particular, how
is talk being used to get things done. Let the last word in this section
be said by a tough young vehicle mechanic, forced to do 'English'
as part of his ONC work at a College of Further Education. His

group met once a week for the whole of Monday afternoon. After three sessions using K4, 'Applying for a job', he turned to the lecturer and said, rank incredulity in his voice,

'Who'd a thought ye could get so bleedin much done, just sittin on yer arse arguin the toss?

## 15 The question of 'correctness' in spoken English

All I ever get out of them are grunts and mutters. They are too lazy to speak properly.

Yes, but are the units going to help them to speak correctly?

Perhaps I could illustrate the very wide range of meaning which these quotations embrace by recalling some of the details of the two conversations with teachers in which they occurred. In the first conversation, I was talking to a senior member of staff from a comprehensive school in North Kent. She approached me with the problem presented by what she called, 'The laziness of pupils who were too careless to speak properly'. I asked what she meant by 'speaking properly' and she explained that all she wanted these pupils to do was to speak clearly and grammatically, in sentences, articulating each word precisely, and thus to give up their dreadful slovenliness, the kind of slovenliness which made them say 'ain't' and 'goin', when they meant 'are not' and 'going'. She argued forcefully that if pupils could not perform the simple task of 'speaking properly' then their intelligence was such that she could not be expected to teach them English. With their own 'impure' version of the language, how could they possibly appreciate great literature?

The second conversation took place in a Teachers' Centre in North Lancashire. The teacher this time was an older woman, responsible for a leaver's class in a big Secondary Modern school in the Rossendale Valley. 'I'm so worried about they way they speak', she began. 'How do you mean?', I asked. 'Well you see, the valley is somewhat enclosed, the children do not have much contact with the outside world and I'm really concerned that if they have to leave the valley, as most of them will, they just won't be understood. They have a way of speaking all their own, I had to learn it when I first came. It took me nearly a year before I could stop asking them to repeat things for me.' The teacher then went on to describe some of the features of her pupils' speech which she felt would cause difficulty, for example, the very large number of words for everyday objects which an outsider

62

could not understand at first hearing, grammatical constructions, particularly the use of tenses and pronouns, specific to the area; and habits of address which might give offence.

This teacher was not concerned about the purity or impurity of her pupils' language, about the acceptability or unacceptability of the way they spoke, but about the fact that the language which was acceptable and effective and suited to all the needs of their life in the valley would cause them great difficulty if they subsequently had to leave the valley to find work, as was highly likely.

Unlike so many of the topics I have considered so far, I cannot now immediately show what the units have to offer to these two teachers, because the problems they present raise issues fundamental to the whole question of how we learn to use language to live. I must ask the reader to follow me on a necessary digression in which I will examine the implications of these ideas about 'correctness' from a linguistic point of view. It is essential to look at the relationship between an individual and his language before formulating an answer to the questions these two teachers posed in terms of what they might do in their own classrooms.

As the reader may imagine, the relationship between the individual human being and his language is a vast subject. For a fully developed account of it he must turn to those titles mentioned in the Postscript on page 112. What follows is, therefore, a brief comment only on the way in which the child learns his language, by the process of using it in the course of his normal existence as a member of a human community. This is the only way to show why many of the popular ideas about 'correctness', as prevalent amongst teachers as amongst anyone else, are so damaging to their pupils. Although these ideas are examined in the context of the child's, or the pupil's, use of *spoken* language, virtually all that is said in this section can be applied equally well to popular ideas about correctness in written language. The problems that are special to written language have been reserved for the next section.

Language is not something that an individual *possesses*, like a dress or a bicycle: it is something which he makes for himself from the resources provided by the environment in which he lives. Essentially, these resources are the patterns of the spoken language he hears about him every day, and the ways of speaking used by the adults with whom he comes in daily contact. Every single undamaged, human infant has the capacity to 'make meanings' for himself out of the language environment into which he is born and a key part of that environment is what is said *to him* and what he hears people say to each other. Whatever language is used to carry on the everyday business of living, and to care for him, is the language he will draw upon in the processes of forming his own ways of speaking; thus the meanings he learns to make as he learns to use language are the meanings existing in his most intimate environment, his family. 'Learnt at my mother's knee' is literally true when we are thinking about the sources of a child's use of language.

As this is the case, there are two critical factors to bear in mind. First, a child can only learn from what is available to him. For example, recently I have spent some time organising reading lessons for a thirty-year-old woman who went to primary school at the age of five unable to speak. She had been cared for since infancy by an elderly grandmother and she had virtually no contact with other children before going to school. At school, she was caned for 'refusing to speak when she was spoken to', and only when she changed schools at eight years old was anything done about her sad plight. At the other end of the scale, a Nigerian colleague of ours has a small daughter, aged four, who speaks one tribal language to her mother, a second tribal language to her father, English to both of them when they are together, and Hausa to her playmates. This child has the opportunity to hear and speak the four languages which are in constant use in her environment, and consequently her experience of using language is very wide for her age. On the other hand, my unfortunate friend, who had only the indistinct mutterings of a weary, old woman to listen to was grossly limited. But *both* individuals share this in common: their capacity to use language effectively has been decisively shaped by the language environment of their early years, years critical for the process of learning one's own language, or languages.

The second factor we must recognise is that what a child learns becomes part of him. The idea of 'possessing' or 'acquiring' language does incline us to think of language as something 'out there', like a commodity, and the habit of talking about 'language acquisition' in educational circles does not help matters. This view of learning language is singularly unfortunate when we are thinking of pupils in schools, because it would then be so easy to ask the pupil to cast aside the old things he has brought into the classroom with him were his language like a dress or a bicycle. It is simply not like this, however.

Consider the passion of any minority group, such as speakers of Welsh, who are anxious to preserve their language. They feel that the loss of their language would be much more to them than the loss of a local way of speaking, for it represents their most intimate experience. Language is not a 'thing': it is the product of lives lived in particular places at particular times. A man's language is the product of all he has experienced, all he has known and done in the world. Language is thus a most intimate part of us, of who we are and what we are, a part just as intimate as our body shape or hair colour. It is the major means we have for shaping our world by making meanings for what we experience of it. The language we speak in going about the normal processes of our day-to-day lives thus stands in a very special relationship to us. What the very idea of 'correctness' introduces, therefore, is an alien valuation of one of our most intimate acts.

Given that this is how we learn and use language, what then are the implications for the teacher's approach to 'correctness'? Does this view of language learning enable us to evaluate current attitudes to 'correctness' in using spoken English as they occur in the context of the school? Does it offer us a viable alternative way of assessing pupils' ways of speaking? Does it suggest an approach which would encourage pupils to develop the range and effectiveness of their ways of speaking once they are in school? In the remainder of this section I suggest that, in each case, the answer must be 'Yes, it does'.

This view of language would suggest, for instance, that the teacher from North Kent was taking a wholly inappropriate view of 'correctness'. Having shown that a pupil's ways of speaking relate to the environment in which he has learnt them it is unreasonable to describe as 'slovenly' ways of speaking which meet most effectively all the needs of the pupil's life outside school. Moreover, a term like 'slovenly' appears to have a large element of the subjective aesthetic response about it and this is surely inappropriate when we are trying to assess pupils' needs. Certainly, the ways of speaking these pupils used may not have been at all suited to the needs of the learning situations with which they were presented, but rejecting the validity of those ways of speaking *in themselves* is surely not a good way to beginning to provide the new ones the pupils now need.

Is there any real difference between calling 'slovenly' children's speech that is unacceptable to your ideas of 'correctness', and calling the child whose speech was non-existent, 'lazy' or 'stupid'? Similarly, can we criticise a pupil for his inability to 'discuss', if the only form of interchange he is familiar with is 'argument' in the sense of violent, personal 'disagreement'? How, for example, can a pupil 'describe' his feelings if he has very little, or possibly no, opportunity to do this in the normal course of his life outside school? How can a pupil be asked to discuss the difficulties of a particular experiment, a typical O-level question, if he has never experienced these difficulties by 'doing' the experiment?

What the pupil brings to school with him is a set of ways of speaking which he has developed to meet his needs *up to that time*. What the school requires of the pupil is that he learn a whole new set of ways of speaking that he does not have at that time. There is no reason why a pupil, who has successfully acquired one set of ways of speaking, should not use the same capacity to acquire others that the school would like him to have, given two conditions: firstly, that he has the same kind of opportunity to make sense of, and to practise, these new ways of speaking as he had in former language learning situations: and secondly, that he has the same *motivation* to learn new ways that he had in those former language learning situations.

Of course, the question of motivation raises in its train the question as to whether or not the ways of speaking he is asked to learn in school are as intrinsically meaningful, as necessary to his survival, as those which he learns in the context of home and community. While this question lies outside the scope of the present book, it has to be said that many teachers do still insist on ways of speaking in their own classrooms that are virtually empty of meaning in any other context, even one provided by the same subject elsewhere in the same school. An example of this is the historian who had worked out so elaborate a system of question and answer to teach what he regarded as 'objectivity' to his first- and second-formers that they had to have their own examination paper, because they could not answer questions set by any other member of the department.

Perhaps this is where we come to the heart of the problem. Whereas teachers do not expect pupils to come to school knowing how to paint, or how to play rugby football, or how to do experiments, they *do* expect pupils to come to school using the kind of language that school activities require. To most teachers, it is obvious that, if pupils talk non-stop in the playground and corridors, then it must be some kind of wilfulness or laziness on their part when they will not talk in class when they are asked to. This is rather like assuming that someone who can play a piano can also play a violin, because they are both musical instruments!

The fact that pupils come to school needing to learn the ways of speaking used by the school, just as they learnt the ways of speaking used by their family, is one aspect of the question of correctness. The other aspect of the question relates to the fact that language is an *intimate* possession, something which can be very seriously damaged if it is abused. For example, if a teacher criticises a pupil's language,

66

commenting on its inappropriateness in the context, its 'slovenliness', or its 'incorrectness', then he is rejecting the pupil's major means for living and for learning and for making himself an individual person. Surely, very few teachers would consider it proper to criticise the shape of a child's nose, or the appearance of his parents, or the colour of his skin, yet many teachers unwittingly make attacks upon a pupil's use of language that are exactly comparable to personal criticism of this kind. They are then puzzled or distressed when pupils respond with one of their two available weapons, withdrawal or rejection.

The next step in our investigation is to look more closely at this idea of a way of speaking and distinguish between two basic elements that go to make it up. The first element is 'speech sound' and the second 'habits of saying'. This distinction is an important one, because the speech sounds we make are very difficult to modify, or to add to, should we want to modify them, while our 'habits of saying' are much easier to modify, or to add to, if we so choose. Let me give two examples to show what I mean. In the course of my field work in the West of Ireland I was frequently faced with Irish English that was not immediately understandable to me. On one occasion a woman answered me by saying, 'Ah, now I can't tell ye that . . . but go down the haggard and Thomas is muggling reeks. He'll tell ye.' This is clearly a dialect form of English. No problem arises from the grammar or the speech sounds. One can see that this sentence will make sense once one has a translation for 'haggard', 'muggling' and 'reeks'. On that occasion, the speaker came to my aid immediately, and said, 'Ah miss, I'm forgettin meself, 'tis our country way of speaking— Thomas is yonder beyond the house on top of the haystack'. The problem this presents to the listener is similar to the problem presented by one of the best-known poems in the language,

Twas brillig and the slithy toves
Did gyre and gimble in the wabe.

Lewis Carroll provided perfectly grammatically well-formed sentences, but he invented his own words. Like the speaker in the West of Ireland, however, the words he used obeyed the rules of English phonology. The verb 'muggle' and the adjective 'slithy' are clearly 'English', in the sense that the Turkish verb 'calisajakdim' and the Nigerian adjective 'ngonga' are not. If we 'cannot understand a word he says', we must be very clear in our minds as to *what* element in the speaker's utterance is causing us difficulty.

This leads me to consider a further, and quite crucial point, which connects this experience of mine in Western Ireland with pupils in classrooms. One of the ways in which human beings use language is to express their feelings towards others. They do this both directly, by saying what they feel, and indirectly, by their use of language towards those people. By finding a new way of speaking which would help me out of my difficulties, the old woman was making a gesture of acceptance. She was accepting that my way of speaking was different, but 'acceptable' and that I was 'friendly'. I was not critical of her, her way of life or her way of speaking, and consequently she responded to my questions with a particular sort of effort, the sort of effort that pupils will indeed make, if they see a need, and if they feel safe from the kind of criticism I have spoken of earlier in this section. At the same time, it is the sort of effort that a teacher must also be prepared to make as a necessary part of doing his job. A teacher should not see a willingness on his own part to 'understand' his pupils' ways of speaking as some kind of 'giving in to them', some 'undermining of academic standards', but rather as a necessary co-operation without which he cannot possibly go on to achieve his objectives. The more necessary the use of a formal technical language is for his work, as in science or mathematics, the more he needs to make the bridge between the pupil's habitual ways of speaking and these radically new ways he wishes him to use.

Let us now go further into this difference between 'speech sound' and 'habits of saying'. Some years ago, my husband got lost in Sheffield one pouring, wet night. Parking his motor scooter, he dripped into a butcher's shop, which still appeared to be open, though it was long after closing time. 'Good evenings' were exchanged and a request for directions was made. A group of three men had dropped in for a chat with the butcher and it was to them that the butcher turned to discuss the problem which the stranger had presented. What my husband said had indeed created problems for the listeners, because he had asked for a district he called 'Lydgate', a district these men knew only as 'Liggit'. They had to decide, first, what the stranger could mean and, having agreed about this, they then had to work out a set of suitable directions. My husband was not able to understand a single word of this conversation. Not only were the speech sounds unfamiliar to a Londoner's ear, but the grammatical structures, and the actual words used, were also unfamiliar. However, when the butcher finally turned back from his consultations his directions were perfectly comprehensible:

Ga on oup ta top of t'ill. . . .

There were three reasons why the directions themselves were comprehensible, when the immediately preceeding conversation had been quite incomprehensible. Firstly, there was goodwill on both sides: both speaker and hearer were making an effort to understand each other in face of difficulties which they intuitively recognised and accepted as valid. Secondly, when the butcher gave the directions, he used the 'common language' as far as grammar and vocabulary were concerned. He did not use the forms he had previously used when talking to his friends. Thirdly, the shopkeeper moved towards the sound patterns of the 'common language' as far as it was possible for him to do.

What we might suggest here is that these men had an 'inside' and and an 'outside' language. Their 'inside' language expresses their habitual and most frequent ways of speaking: it will be used in informal settings such as the context of home and work. The 'outside' language is significantly different. It will be used in more formal situations, such as contact with individuals in public offices, or with management at work, or with people from outside one's own community. Its meanings do not arise from the intimate patterns of a closely shared way of life, and are thus readily usable in a much wider range of contexts than the meanings of the 'inside language'.

There is one sense in which we can say that what the teacher in the Rossendale Valley must do, and indeed what any teacher must do when faced with ways of speaking that will not meet his needs in the classroom, is create conditions in which pupils can develop and practice an appropriate 'outside' language, because 'outside' language, like 'inside' language, can only be learnt in a context that makes its use seem meaningful to the speaker. Let us, therefore, go back now to the problem the teacher from the Rossendale Valley presented to me and look at it in the light of all that I have said about pupils and their language, for her problem is representative of the problem presented by pupils whose habitual ways of speaking constitute an 'inside language' and whose customary way of life gives them little or no opportunity to develop a fluent 'outside language'.

Firstly, it will be clear to the reader that this teacher is in fact in a very good position to help her pupils. Unlike the teacher in North Kent, who is rejecting totally what her pupils bring her, this teacher is not critical of her pupils' ways of speaking and she is not rejecting what they have to offer; she is simply anxious about the limitations which their 'inside language' may impose upon them. Secondly, this teacher does understand both the speech sounds and the habits of speaking of her pupils, because she has listened carefully to them and

69

has considered it a crucial part of her job to understand what they were saying. What she now needs is a way in which she can continuously create situations that will require a use of 'outside language' by these pupils. This is where the units can help, and indeed have helped, because, as I have shown, one of their main features is that they continually put pupils in the position of needing to find new ways of speaking in order to pursue the work they promote. The fact that much of the work of the units is done in small groups would be particularly helpful to the Rossendale teacher, for her pupils are much less likely to feel self-conscious using new words, or new ways of speaking, if they have a chance to practise in small groups with other pupils.

At this point, some readers may feel that a key feature of such schools as the one in the Rossendale Valley is being overlooked. They would argue that it is precisely in such unified 'closed' communities that one cannot 'start where the pupil is', as far as language is concerned, because all they have is their 'inside language' and if you let them work together in groups all they will do is reinforce their use of it and gain nothing new. There are three points to be made about this objection. Firstly, it is not so much that these pupils lack all alternatives to their 'inside' language, but that they have had virtually no opportunity to use 'outside' language. Secondly, the teaching situation, that is, simply being in school, suggests to them that they should move away from 'inside' language towards 'outside' language. Thirdly, the kinds of work the units require of them, especially the need to collaborate in reaching decisions and carrying them out, and the need to present the results of their work to the whole class, or even another class, lie well outside the range of convenience of their customary ways of speaking, so they are very ready to turn to alternative ways of speaking for these tasks.

Finally, it must be said, that whatever strategies the units provide, and however effective they have already proved to be in extending pupils' ways of speaking, their potential is completely dependent on the teacher in one respect. If a teacher firmly believes that, 'They can't speak properly' or that 'They are too lazy to speak properly', then the units can do very little. The exploration of the relationship between a pupil and his language I have offered in this section makes very clear why this should be so and why, therefore, I give only one answer at the end, though I began this section with two problems. The teacher from North Kent had already made up her mind about her pupils. She did not want to be confused with facts, units or alternative ways of seeing the potential which lay in the ways of

70

speaking her pupils could use. In such a case, there is no answer to give.

## 16 The question of 'correctness' in written English

Will the units help me to get them to write 'correctly' . . . and what about their spelling?

In the last section the subject of 'correctness' was discussed at length with particular reference to speech, but it was pointed out that most of what was being said in that section was equally relevant to the question of writing. Let us consider briefly why this is so.

When he goes to school for the first time the major task facing every child is learning a totally new way of using language by making marks on the page. In a literate culture such as ours, learning to read and write is basic for survival. The biggest single handicap to any individual in the normal course of living is an imperfect command of the writing system. The most important thing I have said, however, is that the child has to learn a new *way of using* language. He does not have to learn a new *language* in any true sense of the word. He has to learn how to use his knowledge of the language to make sense of the marks on the page and to produce meaningful marks of his own. For teachers, this distinction is crucial, and the older the pupil the more important it becomes to recognise the fact. When we are talking about pupils in Secondary school and their writing, we are talking about their ability to use language in new ways, not about their need to learn a new language. What I have to say about 'correctness' in writing, therefore, must be read with this fundamental point in mind.

At its simplest, then, what the young child does when he begins to learn how to write is to learn to make the marks on the page that will represent accurately the things he wants to say. How accurately he can connect the form of the words he wants to use with the marks he makes on the page is one aspect of writing that all teachers focus upon. 'Spelling', however, is only *one* aspect of representing the things one wants to say by marks on the page. and it may be that we over-emphasise its relative importance in the total process of using the writing system. When a child writes he uses words which he knows and structures familiar to him in his spoken language. This presents another and much more important aspect, the *form* given to what is written, what we loosely mean by 'grammar'.

Rejecting what a pupil writes as 'incorrect', and therefore 'unacceptable', is just as non-productive as rejecting what he says by calling it 'slovenly' or 'lazy'. Just as rejecting what pupils say is to cut off the very raw material the teacher needs for his work, so rejecting what pupils write sets up a process of ever-diminishing returns, until they are as 'silent' on paper as they can be in the classroom. A teacher cannot 'correct' work which pupils cannot be persuaded to produce, any more than he can develop particular ways of speaking when all his pupils offer him is their silence.

I am very aware here of the dilemma which a statement like this can create for a teacher. Teachers are only too painfully aware that just as judgments are made about pupils' ability, based purely on how they speak, or what kind of accent they have, so judgments about their ability will also be made purely on their ability to spell, to write neatly, or to punctuate correctly. In these circumstances, a teacher is sorely tempted to 'correct' every 'mistake' which 'could be taken down and used as evidence against them', the 'them' in this case being, directly, the pupil, but indirectly, the teacher himself. At the same time, most teachers are aware that continuous correction can so discourage pupils that they refuse to write anything at all, because they feel that putting anything down on paper only leaves them open to criticism. What is the teacher to do?

I want to suggest that there is a strong parallelism between the situation with writing and the situation with speaking which I outlined in the last section. Just as a pupil brings 'habits of speaking' into the classroom which are effective in one context, but not in another, so, in the same way, pupils bring 'habits of writing' into the classroom which are effective in some contexts, but may be limiting in others. Just as a pupil can find new ways of speaking to meet particular needs, however, so he can develop new habits of writing to meet new needs, given that he has the motivation and the chance to practise these new ways. What would help our discussion at this point is to make a distinction between 'correctness' and 'accuracy'. Let me recount an incident which illustrates this distinction and at the same time the dilemma which teachers face over the question of 'correctness'. Recently a colleague of ours supervised a student on teaching practice in a Junior school in South Lancashire. The student was a capable one and the children were working well, but when our colleague arrived to visit his student he found her both worried and apologetic. 'They really are quite bright children', she explained, 'but they keep making spelling mistakes in simple words.' Our colleague collected some of the children's work and found that indeed on a piece of work about 'Money', not a single child had spelt the word 'money' accurately, according to the rules of the standard

72

orthography, although most of them had been accurate in their spelling of 'pence' and 'pound' and 'pocket'. The explanation for this was readily discoverable. The student herself, together with all the teachers in the school, as well as the children themselves, all pronounced the word 'money', as 'mu̟ney', using a form of the word common to this part of South Lancashire. Far from 'getting it wrong', the six-year-olds in this class had all produced a correct, orthographic representation of the word which they knew as 'mu̟ney'. It took a Norfolk-born supervisor, with a different form for this vowel, to spot the fact that the children's systematic 'mis-spellings' were mostly the product of local pronunciation *correctly* rendered.

What the children produced was 'correct', according to the relationship between the sounds they spoke and the marks they made on the page, but not 'accurate' to the rules of the standard orthography for making relationships between sound and letter. Similarly, the grammatical forms which some pupils use can be 'correct, but non-standard'. The Rossendale Valley pupils produced writing full of such forms. So was the writing of many of the pupils in the Belfast schools that I knew. Consider this example. Walking behind a mill girl in a crowded Belfast street one day, I overheard the following statement:

And my Mammy, when she foun out, she was mad at me, so she was, hey.

Looking at the work of girls from a Secondary Modern in East Belfast, later that week, I found, 'I did do it and my teacher when she found out she was mad at me, so she was!'. The one concession to the written mode is that the girl has dropped any written representation for that highly expressive verbal gesture, 'Hey', and substituted, accurately, an exclamation mark. The whole sentence had been crossed out and 'ungrammatical' written in the margin. There was no comment from the teacher to suggest the girl had been able to convey meaning unambiguously and with feeling.

This is what I meant when I suggested earlier that, just as a pupil brings to school with him 'habits of speaking' that are effective in one context but not necessarily so in every context he might meet, so a pupil reflects these 'habits of speaking' in what he writes, and thus what he writes, while effective in one context, will not meet the needs of all the contexts in which he will find himself having to write. The form the Belfast girl used in her piece was wholly acceptable in terms of her account of her personal experience, but would be much less so were it to occur in such a context as a public examination:

> Archbishop Becket did do it and the King when he found out he was mad at him so he was.

Our six-year-olds' rendering of 'money' is in fact 'correct' and effective, and perfectly adequate for everyday personal communication in the context of their school and community, just as their pronunciation of 'money' is 'correct' and effective in that context, but at the same time this is not an *accurate* representation of the standard form of the language. Now if teachers are committed to developing pupils' capacity to produce an *accurate* representation of the standard language, as most teachers seem to be, then the distinction between 'correctness' and 'accuracy' is an important one. Accepting what a pupil writes on a piece of paper as 'correct' in the sense of 'acceptable' does not mean that one is accepting it as 'accurate', but accepting what pupils manage to produce 'correctly' is the first step towards their being able to write 'accurately'. The teacher who rejects the ill-spelt representation of an unfamiliar way of speaking, put on paper in an ill-formed, because unpractised hand, is indeed stopping at source the raw material out of which more accurate forms can grow. When I taught Geography, in both Secondary Modern and Grammar schools, one of my biggest problems was to convince my pupils that they actually *could* write. Pupils who ended up by producing for me splendid, ten-page, illustrated folders on a country or topic of their choice would protest vigorously at the beginning of the activity that they 'couldn't write'. Often, it was pupils who would be described as 'above average' in ability who were the most reluctant, for it was they who had suffered most from the anxieties of their teachers and their parents, focused exclusively as they were on 'the examination'.

Given that most teachers do want to help their pupils towards a more accurate representation of the standard language, how can this 'more accurate representation' be developed? There seem to be three main elements involved. Firstly, a context must be created in which pupils *need* to write as part of some activity which will really engage them. Secondly, what they write must be necessary to the work of another individual or group, so that they have a local 'audience' for its production: and thirdly, there must be some 'public' end-product of the work so that they are required to think of their 'audience' in less directly personal terms. These conditions create a demand for written language which is 'outside language'. They ask the pupil to change his existing way of writing and, in this, these situations for

74

writing parallel the situations for speaking outlined in the last section. As did those situations for speaking, the situations for writing rely upon the units to create an awareness of the need for more accurate forms of writing, the opportunity to try out what is necessary in the local and particular context of the small working group, and the time to practise 'getting it right' before exposing the final result to a 'public' audience, be it the whole class or the teacher himself.

It is conditions of this kind which the units of *Language in Use* create for *both* speaking and writing. For example, the early stages of a unit very often require the collection of material, material which has to be written down, like slang expressions, or observations about the use of language in notices, or ways of addressing people, or lists of jobs done by respective members of a family. This material has to be written down so that it can be shared with other members of a group who are going to *use* it. The actual shared use of written material is a crucial part of this whole process of working towards more accurate forms of the written language, because it is only when written material has to be used that the 'necessity' for accuracy is revealed, and this accuracy relates not only to the meaning but also to the spelling, to the punctuation and to the handwriting used in a text. As one teacher remarked in a report on his work with the units,

'I can't read this', said or written by a friend has far more effect than a gallon of my red ink.

If misspelling, bad handwriting, or ambiguous, or non-existent, punctuation mean that work is held up, then pupils become aware of why standard ways of doing things are necessary. They no longer see 'spelling' and 'punctuation' as something inflicted upon them for its own sake, for no apparent reason other than that 'teacher says': nor do they see it as something one does as 'exercises', to be got 'right' or 'wrong', like 'doing sums', independent of anything to do with creating accurate written text for oneself. Pupils come to see this accuracy as something similar to the rules for a team game. They know as well as anybody that the game is only possible so long as you know and practise the rules in the way you play it. If everybody spells as they want, you have to ask them what they mean. As I have said in other sections, 'If pupils can *see* what is needed, they can very often *do* it': what matters is creating a situation in which they can *see* for themselves what is needed. Drills, like 'telling them how to do it', have very little effect, and for the same reason, for the necessity for being accurate has not been experienced.

If pupils engaged on a piece of work do modify each other's writing at an early stage, in this way, why then is it necessary to proceed to what I have called 'some public end-product of the work'? There are two reasons. Firstly, the quality of the work, and the pupils' involvement in it, is profoundly influenced at the early stages by what the ultimate objective is. A group of twelve-year-olds preparing for a classroom display on a topic they have chosen will be far more involved in the work, and demand a far higher standard of work from each other, than twelve-year-olds who are working on something which, like the weekly essay of a young friend of mine, will be returned without comment, bearing in red the sole cipher 'Very fair' or 'Quite good'. Secondly, it is the 'public' display of work itself that contributes greatly to creating an understanding of the need for accuracy. If pupils are really involved in what they are doing, particularly where they are using books and magazines and other printed matter, they begin to compare what they themselves are producing with what they see around them. Having an idea of what the finished product, be it magazine, newsheet, report or wall display will look like, is a very important part of being able to produce it. Unless what pupils produce is to have a wider audience than themselves, they will not make comparisons of this kind, and consequently they are unlikely to develop new models for presenting their work or the feeling for accuracy that goes with them.

There is one further point to be made about this concept of 'accuracy'. The level of accuracy necessary for a text is not always the same. For example, it is quite immaterial to me if I go shopping with a misspelt shopping list. It is equally unimportant to me if I find a note in the kitchen reminding me to 'Check the carburretta' or to 'Soke the lentils'. As long as the instruction conveys its *meaning*, the *accuracy* of its *expression* seems to me unimportant. The circumstances change, however, when we move from 'private' to 'public'. Whereas my shopping list relates only to me, the letter I write to a grant-awarding body regarding research funds is quite a different matter, as is the misplaced comma in the manuscript I have just proof read. Very many pupils are offered no significant differentiation between texts. At one level, there are pupils whose very 'shopping lists' are corrected; at another, there are pupils who do not see any difference between what goes up on the wall for the whole class to see and what remains in their jotter. What the units do very successfully is to create a kind of 'hierarchy' of using ways of writing which move progressively from most private to most public and therefore from 'least need for accuracy' to 'most need for accuracy'. Pupils do appear to respond to this as one would expect, by making progressively greater demands upon each other for accuracy the more public the text is to be. What helps this process is that all of the writing required by the units arises out of some specific activity: it is *for* something and not merely requested as a thing in itself unrelatable to any real context of experience. This is the other factor which affects pupils' evaluation of the text they produce. If a text is the product of their own thought and effort, and a contribution to the work of the group, it is automatically rated higher in terms of the degree of accuracy required than some piece of writing which appears to have no relationship to them.

# V Units in the English class

## 17 Do the units help with the teaching of literature?

*But if I did all that we'd never get any books read.*

The comment which heads this section was made by a Head of English in a big Secondary Modern school in the Midlands. He had been sent a copy of the trial version of *Language in Use* and asked for his comments on it. When he returned the book to the project team he wrote a long letter explaining that while he found the units interesting and worth while he felt he could not give up all his other activities in their favour. Like some of the teachers we spoke to on our travels who felt that they must give up all their habitual ways of teaching and do only what the units recommend, this Head of Department, too, felt that there was some sort of either/or involved in taking up *Language in Use*.

*Language in Use*, however, is a resource, something which is offered to the teacher to use as he wishes, and when he wishes, in developing any aspect of his work for which the use of a unit might strike him as relevant. It is not a course book which has to be begun at the beginning and worked through systematically to the end in order to get anything out of it. *Language in Use* contains so many units just because it must give the teacher the range of choice he needs in view of the variety of his concerns and it can only do this by presenting a great deal of material to choose from. Indeed, it is precisely because of the variety of things teachers of English want to do that the range the units offer can be so useful to them.

Does this range extend to work with literature, however? Like so many things in teaching, the answer depends upon what one regards as 'literature', and how one intends to teach it. It is common knowledge that there are wide differences of opinion amongst teachers of English as to what the word 'literature' means and how it should be taught. For some teachers, 'literature' is the set books of an A-level syllabus and 'teaching' means a detailed literary critical study. For others, 'literature' means any printed matter that their pupils are capable of reading and understanding, limited as they are either by their ability to read or their limited experience of the world. What all teachers of English seem to be in agreement about is that helping

78

pupils to make a relationship with books, plays and poems is a key part, some would say the most important part, of their work.

What I want to suggest is that, whatever one's individual view of literature and its part in the work of the English class, the units are likely to have something useful to offer. Far from taking up time which otherwise might have been devoted to literature, the units have been used by many teachers to expand and develop their work with literature. By using units to focus pupils' attention on what they themselves know about the world around them, teachers have been able to 'sensitise' pupils to aspects of novels, stories or poems which they might otherwise not have been able to understand. In fact, this 'sensitising', this awakening of pupils' responsiveness to something in a text they would otherwise overlook, was what our colleague in Belfast was doing when he used 'National Characteristics' (see p. 42). In this sense, the way in which teachers have used the units to develop pupils' sensitivity towards what is going on in novels or stories or plays is analogous to the way in which the units develop pupils' awareness of how they use language for living and learning. In fact, the two things are very closely related, for one major barrier between pupils and the literature their teachers would like them to read is their lack of awareness of alternative ways of using language from the ways familiar to them in their own community. The reader may remember that on the occasion described on page 43, a group of boys were using this unit to develop their ideas about the characteristics of foreigners and the idea of stereotypes. They discussed the difference between 'a stage Irishman', and Irishmen as they had experienced them in their own everyday lives. The reader can imagine for himself how this discussion was then used when the following week the boys met George Orwell's essay, 'Boys' Weeklies'.

Using a unit as a 'way-in' to a particular story, novel or play has been widely employed. It appears to be particularly successful with the kind of pupil who is highly resistant to reading anything at all on the grounds that it is 'only a story'; or that it is 'not true to life'; or that it is 'only about olden days'. For example, a teacher in a big girls' selective school in Nottingham found herself faced with the prospect of teaching *Hamlet* to a class taking A-level. The teacher, who herself had been born in the area where the girls lived, knew that she would meet a very strong resistance to the idea of reading *Hamlet*, for she was familiar with the attitudes towards drama, art and poetry in the community. Her predictions were fulfilled, for her pupils engaged reluctantly with the text, willing only to tolerate such 'poncy', 'out-of-date' stuff for the sake of the examination. At this point, the teacher decided to use unit H3, 'Playing many parts', a unit which explores the fact that we each of us have a number of parts to play in our everyday lives and that we have to develop appropriate ways of speaking in order to play these parts. For example, at any one time a female can be simultaneously wife and mother, daughter and granddaughter, sister and sister-in-law, friend, neighbour, patient, teacher, consumer, road-user, etc. What the unit sets out to do is to:

> explore the crucial part played by language in both the exercise and the identification of roles. What we say to the other person and how we say it, and what is said to us in reply, provide the major means by which we judge what kind of relationship is involved and what our part in it is expected to be.

The choice of unit was a very skilful one, for the teacher in question knew her pupils well and she knew that they would respond to thinking about the different relationships they themselves entered into. They did indeed respond in this way and their new perception of relationships was not set aside when *Hamlet* was resumed. In particular, a study of Claudius throughout the play brought home to them the fact that there was little difference between Elizabethans and Moderns as far as the rapid assumption of different roles was concerned, and that these changes of role gave the clue to Claudius as a character in the action of the play. While some girls still announced loudly that it was still 'poncy', the majority now saw that it was possible to relate the apparently remote and alien world of *Hamlet* to aspects of their own experience. With this test of the 'truthfulness' of the play, they were then much more willing to face the difficulties presented by the real differences between Hamlet's world and way of thinking and our own. Like my own work with A-level geographers, the fact that it *was* A-level is really incidental to the point I want to make. This work with *Hamlet* is just as typical of the way the units have been used to lead into a text, whatever the age or ability of the pupils, as the geographer's work on 'audience' was typical of the way the units have been used to encourage growth of awareness.

Working in a quite different context with twelve-year-olds, two teachers used units to develop their work with James Vance Marshall's *Walkabout*. *Walkabout* is the story of two American children, a girl of thirteen and a boy of about eight, who are the only survivors of an aircrash in the Australian desert. They are guided to civilisation by an aborigine boy without whose skill at living off the land they could not have survived. There are, however, underlying tensions. The girl is horrified because the aborigine boy is black and is wearing no clothes. At one point in the story the boy expects the girl to carry a parcel. This she rejects as 'his job'. One of the two teachers used units H5, 'Keeping up appearances', and F4, 'National Characteristics', as a preparation for the book, while the other teacher used both these units, together with F2, 'Man's job/woman's work', *after* her pupils had read the book, in order to provide a framework for the ensuing discussion. In both cases, the teachers felt that pupils had benefited from the added understanding which the units had contributed to the reading and the discussion.

Connecting pupils' own experience of life with the characters and events of literature by using units seems to have proved successful in a very wide variety of circumstances; for example, a group of bottom stream boys and girls in a London Comprehensive used F8, 'Slang', before reading parts of Willis Hall's *The Long and the Short and the Tall*, a class of eleven-year-olds used K1, 'Schools and Colleges', and K2, 'School Traditions', to explore the difficulties of a young uninitiated wizard in Chapter 3 of Ursula le Guinn's, 'A Wizard of Earthsea'; and a group of A-level pupils used F10, 'Regional speech', and F11, 'How writers exploit regional speech', in their study of D. H. Lawrence's dialogue in *Sons and Lovers*.

Teachers of English have used units, not only to help their pupils find a way into literature, but also to develop cohesion between the various activities and pieces of work which the reading of literature gives rise to. One teacher used three units, H5, 'Keeping up appearances', H3, 'Playing many parts', and J2, 'How adults see teenagers', grouped together to provide what he called 'a compendium of local objectives'. This gave him a kind of scaffolding within which he could organise very diverse material round a common theme. In this case, he used the role speech from *As You Like It* and Falstaff's 'honour' speech from Henry IV, part 1, in conjunction with material as diverse as the lyrics of current pop songs, teenage magazines and a selection of contemporary poetry. It was this teacher who said that:

> there was reading and writing to teach, there were the newspapers and contemporary culture to discuss, there were habits of reading to inculcate, there were new methods of working to be discovered or imposed, there was Shakespeare to be introduced and poets to be read and so on . . .

but that 'used flexibly, the units could accommodate and provide motive for almost anything I find it necessary to cover'. Far from taking up the time that he wished to devote to the activities he considered important, the units had enabled him to do rather more of what he wanted to do by helping him to think through his objectives, and by providing a framework within which he could have order and pattern without losing the flexibility of action which he valued so highly.

There is one final point to make. While we have been intrigued and fascinated by the wide range of uses to which teachers of English have put the units, it is fair to say that there is seldom a direct or 'obvious' link between the unit itself and work with literature which one can see just by looking at the printed unit on the page. For example, on one occasion a colleague of ours visited a classroom where he knew that a young teacher was using A13, 'Sports commentating'. As he slipped into a seat at the back of the room he was somewhat puzzled by the fact that the record to which the class was listening so intently was one of the newly acquired set of records of *Julius Caesar*. As he listened, he recognised the Forum scene. When the teacher took the record off, it became clear that the discussion on sports reporting had led to a consideration of crowd behaviour at football matches. The boys had pointed out that it only required a small group on the terraces to start shouting 'Off, Off', for a whole section of the crowd to take up the chant. The teacher had taken the opportunity thus presented to play this record of the Forum scene in order to develop the class's ideas about the way crowds can be controlled. Similarly, using 'Man's job/woman's work' with a novel about survival in the Australian desert is not immediately suggested by the unit itself!

What many teachers have pointed out to us is that the better you know the units the more the possibilities present themselves. Once you have thought through 'Man's job/woman's work', and seen its potential for sharpening awareness of how language can be a vehicle for our deepest assumptions about the world, it becomes a standing option should this aspect of reality present itself. It is ready to connect with a whole range of work from a thematic exploration of 'Women's Lib.' to a study of Edna O'Brien or Virginia Woolf. As one teacher summed it up in a report from a study group:

In conclusion, it must be recorded that familiarity with the units is essential. This can only be gained by using them. A quick read through is insufficient. It has been found that, as familiarity with the units increased, so the possibilities for their use was seen to be continually extending. Gradually, parts of the units or knowledge gained through working them began to infiltrate into all aspects of the teaching situation, often to the enlightenment of the teacher and the benefit of pupils.

## 18  Do the units offer scope for drama work?

One of the happiest results of our work with the units was the number of occasions when units led directly to spontaneous improvisations.

Out of the 110 units in *Language in Use*, some twenty-five actually suggest the planning of sketches or the making of a script for acting as part of the work of the unit. In practice, teachers have found that many of the units lend themselves to the setting up of improvisation, if the teacher decides that is the way he wants the class to go. This is particularly the case with units where the focus is upon the particular way in which individuals use language in the context of social relationships, such as, J3, 'Crowds', or J8, 'Being interviewed', or D13, 'Preaching', or K3, 'Negotiating'.

On the other hand, many of the units focus on pupils' experience of the adult world, and it is very easy to move from discussion to improvisation, because what pupils have observed about the world for themselves comes into sharp focus during the course of the unit. For example, one young drama specialist, who also taught English, was already working on the theme of 'Conflict' in her English lessons with a fourth-form class when she began using the units. She decided to explore some of the units in 'Language in Individual Relationships', beginning with H1, 'Family names'. Within a short time she found that more and more 'family' conflicts were being offered as the substance of work in her parallel drama classes with the same form. Eventually her class suggested to her that they might produce some scenes 'to show what happens when people call each other different things'. One group produced a very bitter little scene in which a mother, wanting to persuade her daughter to do something, begins by calling her 'darling', and then 'dear'. As she meets resistance, she moves to 'Paddy', then to 'Pat', and ultimately to 'Patricia'. In the final sequence, after Patricia has been sent to her room, father enters and Patricia is then referred to as 'her ladyship'. After this piece of work this teacher said that the units had helped her pupils to find a way of organising their very accurate observation of adult behaviour by providing a framework within which they were able to improvise with great ease and very little self-consciousness.

For many teachers who want to encourage drama work, especially with adolescents, this self-consciousness can be a major handicap. They find that, while first- and second-year pupils will improvise quite happily, older pupils do become very self-conscious and inhibited when asked to do so on a general theme. The units often use improvisation as a way of presenting evidence about a particular aspect of using language. In this case, pupils do not regard the work as 'drama', because it arises out of the context of the enquiry they are interested in pursuing, and they enter into it without any of the self-consciousness that they otherwise would have displayed. For example, a fourth-year class, for whom enacting had become virtually impossible, were working on H10, 'Taking a hint'. They were asked to write outline sketches for three situations in which a character finds that he has to disguise his feelings, but only partially. The sketches revealed great insight into the way people 'drop hints' and considerable ingenuity in presenting their view of adult ways of behaving. From the teacher's point of view, however, the more important fact was that her fourth-formers were acting again for the first time in months without the awkwardness and inhibition that had led her to abandon this kind of work.

Teachers who make a particular use of drama in order to get to know their pupils better have said that the units have helped them to reach important ideas and attitudes their pupils hold which they had not previously been willing or able to reveal. For example, a teacher who felt it essential to his work that he knew about the home environment of his pupils always tried to focus his first-year pupils on the family and gave plenty of scope for the kind of improvisation that would allow these pupils to reveal something of their background. He had always found that this was a worthwhile activity and that those pupils responded well to the work, but when he used J7, 'Family talk', he found that he was offered a far more detailed and revealing picture than he had ever had before. Working with the unit had enabled his pupils to see that there were more things worth saying, more details which were relevant to the work than they realised. What this class put in were things that other classes in previous years had left out, not through shyness or reticence, but through their very familiarity, their 'obviousness'. The other classes, quite literally, could not 'see' these things were at all worth representing in their work.

The expression of pupils' attitudes through improvisation is considered by many teachers to be one of the very few means by which many of their most deeply held attitudes can be brought into the classroom legitimately, so that they can become the focus for exploration, discussion and perhaps, reconsideration in the light of alternative ways of looking at the same things. Many units are concerned with attitudes, either directly or indirectly, and the example I give below illustrates how important the exploration of attitudes through drama can be, not only in the work of the English teacher, but for those of his colleagues who cannot use such means because of the limitations imposed upon their subject disciplines.

The unit J4, 'Social talk', was being used, not this time with a group of pupils, but with a group of teachers during a 'workshop' at the York International Conference in 1971. The teacher conducting the session created a situation in which small groups of teachers were asked to perform a brief sketch involving the use of 'social talk'. The contexts for the sketches were defined, e.g., a bus stop in the early morning, when the bus is very late; a dentist's waiting room, and so on. The participants were also defined, e.g., middle-aged housewife, schoolgirl, business man. The teachers presented a number of sketches and then turned to consider what particular patterns of language use tended to appear and what topics of conversation were considered suitable. The teachers appeared to find the unit interesting and discussion moved towards the teachers' own interest in using the unit with their pupils. It was at this point that a low-pitched, Scottish voice entered the discussion to point out that he would not be able to use this unit with *his* pupils. The statement produced a certain puzzlement among the assembled teachers. The Scottish teacher explained that if any of his pupils were asked to enact the situation at the bus stop, they would react by producing complete silence, because this would be their experience of that particular situation. Further discussion was impossible because the session had to end, but afterwards I sought out the Scottish teacher. I, too, had been very puzzled by the apparent ease with which complete strangers began to talk to each other about buses and the weather. It was not something I had experienced in my own community in Northern Ireland, and I was anxious to question my Scottish colleague. We found ourselves in immediate agreement, for according to the attitudes of our respective communities, communities which are closely related historically, 'People should not talk unless they have something to say', and 'There's no use talking for the sake of talking'. With these two attitudes underlying pupils' experience, what could either the Scottish teacher or myself expect from this unit other than silence?

I think the most important point to make, however, is that this unit was able to reveal the fact that behaviour in a simple everyday situation like a queue at a bus stop is governed by deeply held attitudes as to whether one ought to use language and what kinds of language are usable. The particular attitude revealed on this occasion, 'Speak only when you have something worth saying', has very important implications for the classroom, especially if the view of 'talk' advanced in the previous chapters is accepted by the reader as valid. Consider for a moment how this attitude is going to affect the pupil in the learning situation. I would suggest, first, that it is going to make him very reluctant to say *anything* he is not absolutely sure about; and secondly, that he is likely to dismiss any kind of exploratory talk or discussion as a waste of time. He may also dismiss a great deal of important activity in school as 'talking for the sake of talking', *if he does not see immediately where it leads to*.

Discovering an attitude such as we have just described may well be critically important for a teacher's approach to drama work, for, indeed, it may help to explain past 'failures', occasions where the teacher could not carry out what seemed a reasonable piece of work, because he was not aware of the built-in attitudes towards language and its use his pupils brought into the classroom or drama studio with them.

## 19  Do the units allow for 'personal writing'?

Teachers of English mean many different things when they use the expression 'personal writing'; for some teachers, it means almost any writing that the pupil does in the context of the English class; to others it means a particular kind of 'creative' or 'imaginative' writing, a particular kind of intimate exploration of individual response which they consider vital to the growth of an individual's awareness of himself and of the world, but which they do not expect teachers of other subjects to understand or encourage. What all teachers of English do seem to agree on is that, somewhere among all their other activities, they must create opportunities for pupils to write in a way that *they*, the pupils, choose for themselves about subjects or situations which they see as important to them. By this means pupils can gain confidence in expressing their thoughts, and especially their feelings, on paper, and, at the same time, shape their feelings and attitudes about the world around them. Many teachers of English now put such emphasis upon this aspect of their work, because they believe work in no other subject can give pupils the same scope for writing in this way. It is this meaning of 'personal writing' which underlies what I have to say about the units in this section.

The short answer to the question, 'Do the units allow for "personal writing"?', is 'Yes, they not only allow for it, but they encourage it'. Why is this so? Part of the answer lies in the fact that the units draw so extensively on a pupil's own experience. If he becomes involved in an exploration of 'Family talk', or 'Taking a hint', he has to focus very sharply upon these particular areas of his experience. He must consider his family and the kind of interchanges which take place within it. He must consider tactfulness, his own, and that of others, and the effect that a lack of tact on his own or someone else's part may create. What this does is to bring into sharp focus for him experience which was certainly there, but which he had not noticed. Although it *was* experience for him, it had remained inert, because he had not been aware that he had it.

Very often, teachers have asked pupils to explore this new-found experience that is yet so familiar to them, through writing stories and poems about it in words of the pupil's own choosing. Just as the units have shown the way into literature which pupils otherwise would not have attempted, so they have led to personal writing which otherwise would not have occurred.

Very often the new insights which develop during the working of a unit are expressed through talk and discussion; often, as we saw in the last section, these insights will emerge as a result of dramatic work like improvisation; but for many pupils it is the personal writing which comes at the end of the exploration that provides the most satisfying way of summing up for themselves what they have gained in awareness. Whether or not they are offered the opportunity to do this rests entirely in the hands of the teacher, for he decides if there is time for this activity. In fact, with this end in view, many teachers have deliberately chosen particular units in order to explore areas of their experience over-familiar to them. For example, one teacher we know used J8, 'Being interviewed', with a group of boys, hoping that the writing it produced might reveal some of the worries which he knew this particular class of leavers certainly had. Throughout the whole sequence of work this teacher encouraged the boys to write about their feelings towards the future, finding a job and starting work, and it was from the information that this personal writing gave him that he developed a programme of work with the units, including K4, 'Applying for a job', K5, 'Starting work', and K7, 'Letters', which helped the boys to prepare for the situations which were worrying them. In particular, one boy's anxieties led him to a sequence of work with the units he would never otherwise have considered with this group. The boy was not very successful at writing stories, but on this occasion he produced a very sharply seen piece about a boy who lost his job because he 'couldn't talk proper'. As a result, the teacher was able to do a great deal to help his class by using C3, 'Distinctive voices', C4, 'Accent', and C5, 'What is speech?'.

Although the individual units themselves may create a great impetus to write personally, simply by making pupils feel easy and self-confident about expressing themselves on paper, some teachers have found that the actual ways of working used in the units seem to encourage this writing by producing new situations in which pupils feel the need to review some part of their common experience. This is something I experienced myself in the context of my work with geography. Very often, I was able to find some time for a class to write personally though the reader will appreciate that it would have been easier if I had been part of a team where an 'English' colleague could have used more time to develop fully the situation which had arisen. Two examples will show what happened. On the first occasion, a third-form group had prepared work for a first-year group and a joint session had been organised, so that the third years could present their work to them and ask the first years to comment upon it. They wanted to know if they had fulfilled successfully the task they had been given, 'To write for a first-form audience'. The joint session was very difficult. Basically, the first-formers were 'shy', they were quite uncharacteristically quiet, and when questioned by the third-formers about the text in front of them, they smiled politely and said nothing. The third form had a difficult time and got very frustrated. When the first-formers had left, the discussion was animated: 'They wouldn't say anything, they just *sat* there'; 'We tried to put our questions nicely and simply, but they wouldn't answer'; 'I think they were afraid they might say the wrong thing'; 'We couldn't find out what they didn't understand, because they wouldn't admit *anything*'.

The discussion was curtailed by the bell, but I asked the girls if they would write for me, in any form they chose, their comments or impressions or thoughts about the afternoon's experience. The results were quite fascinating. Many of the girls tried to work out what caused the 'shyness' of the first-formers, how they had tried to over-come the barrier which it created, and what had happened in the cases where they had failed to overcome it. Some girls began to see 'shyness' as a defence against an unfamiliar or uneasy situation and reflected upon how they themselves 'used' shyness and in what situations. Many of the class had taken up a point I had made in discussion when I asked them to consider what it was like for a teacher, or a student teacher, to encounter the situation they had just experienced. One girl suggested that the antidote to shyness was 'interest'. As she put it: 'If you act shy in school the teacher will choose someone else and you won't have to do whatever it is she wants. But if you were at a party, you wouldn't act shy, for if you did you might miss something that was going on that you were interested in.' There was not a dull piece in the whole set and the writing covered a very great range of thought and mood, from a particular focus on the original situation to speculation about, 'How I must seem to a teacher'. It also had a quality which every teacher must value, it was written with obvious enjoyment.

The second occasion was somewhat different. A very able first-year class was involved in a situation not unlike the one I have already described. This time, however, a fourth-form group were producing work for the first years on 'Deserts'. It was not possible to bring the two classes together, face-to-face, so I asked the first years to make written criticism of the work which I would give to the fourth years. This was duly done, but I was disturbed to find that the criticisms were rather unconstructive and indeed often hurtful. I did not pass them on immediately and I was wondering what to do, when the first-year class raised the subject of criticism themselves. Had I passed on their criticisms? Were the fourth-formers annoyed? I asked them if they thought the fourth-formers should be annoyed and this led us to discuss 'criticism'. The class had had second thoughts; they had done the work according to what they understood by the word 'criticise'. In their community, 'to criticise' was a very forceful and wholly destructive activity. They now realised what they had done and they regretted it. In the personal writing which followed they considered the reasons for the style of their original criticism, reviewed this, suggested possible alternatives, and explored their own personal reactions to 'being criticised', an activity which gave me a great deal of information about their families, their teachers and their attitudes to many things.

When I compare the things *said* in discussion with the things individual girls *wrote*, it seemed to me essential that the opportunity for personal writing is made available as a normal part of work with a unit if the fullest use is to be made of all that the unit gives rise to. Similarly, I would suggest that when the units are used to develop a dramatic exploration of the attitudes and assumptions which pupils bring to school, then there is just as much need to use personal writing in support of the dramatic activity. It is clear from both the examples given and from the comments of many other teachers, that there are things arising out of dramatic work with the units which pupils can shape best in writing that is personal and in a form of their own choosing.

## 20 Can the units help with a 'thematic' approach?

In Section 17, when I was talking about units and literature, I referred to a teacher who used a group of units, H5, 'Keeping up appearances', H3, 'Playing many parts', and J2, 'How adults see teenagers', to provide for himself a framework for the work he wanted to do. I can put this another way and say that he had chosen a theme, 'How we see people', and he had chosen these units specifically to give himself and his pupils the scope they needed for an exploration of what this theme involved.

The units have been used extensively by teachers for theme-based work of this kind and in this section I shall give some examples of the way in which this has been done. There are three basic ways in which the units help with theme-based work: firstly, they can be used as they are and put together to develop a theme which a teacher already has in mind; secondly, a unit, or a group of units, can be used to create a theme which is then explored, perhaps through further units, or by the use of other means such as novels, plays, films or television. Thirdly, individual units can be used to provide links between the elements of a theme.

Let us first consider units grouped so as to provide the basis for the exploration of a particular theme. This kind of grouping has been used in a wide variety of contexts. For example, a teacher in a selective girls' school used five units to explore the theme of 'Choosing one's words'. The five units used were, H3, 'Playing many parts', H9, 'Being tactful', H10, 'Taking a hint', B1, 'Formal and informal', and B8, 'Persuasion'. The girls she was working with were fifteen-year-olds and were reading that year, *Hamlet*, *Emma*, and *Sons and Lovers*, as part of their O-level course. By choosing this theme and these units this teacher was able to integrate her necessary literature teaching with a variety of other activities which included improvisation, a study of advertising and teenage magazines, and a study of ways of writing, including letter writing. In a very different setting, a group of thirteen-year-olds in a Secondary Modern school tackled, 'Words and how we use them', with the help of these five units: D2, 'Order in sentences', A9, 'New words', C5, 'What is speech?', A10, 'Observing and describing', and B8, 'Persuasion'. In both these sequences, units have been drawn freely from any section of *Language in Use* that seemed relevant and they were chosen so as to meet the specific needs of a particular learning situation. In some cases, such themes grow by their own momentum and lead to the use of further units. For example, the selective school teacher used K7, 'Letters', because the opportunity to do so had arisen from B1, 'Formal and informal', where the discussion had come to centre upon the problem of formality in writing letters.

Some sequences of units used to build up a theme have drawn on all three parts of *Language in Use*. For example, a group of eighteen-year-olds in a sixth-form college used D1, 'Sounds, words and meanings', D5, 'What is a rule?', E4, 'Half, please', H5, 'Keeping up appearances', and E3, 'Reticence', to explore, 'The Rules of Language', in both senses of the word 'rule'. 'Learning the rules', was taken up as a theme by two teachers working in very different situations. The first teacher, working with eleven-year-olds, newly arrived in a big Secondary Modern school, used K1, 'Schools and colleges', K2, 'School traditions', J1, 'Belonging to a group', B4, 'Notices', and D7, 'Expecting the usual', to help them come to terms with their new environment, while the other teacher, working with twenty-year-old day release apprentices, used K4, 'Applying for a job', J8, 'Being interviewed', B1, 'Formal and informal', and K7, 'Letters' to explore the rules governing the new situations which they would soon be encountering at the end of their apprenticeship.

The themes which I have outlined above as examples of how the units can be used do not include any from the group of themes most popular with teachers of English, themes like 'Family', or 'Conflict', or 'Growing up'. This is because the Unit Index from *Language in Use* is reprinted at the back of this volume and any teacher who consults it will see for himself how many units there are that would fit into any theme with a personal or a social dimension of this kind.

It seems that the use of a single unit is often the beginning of a theme, particularly in those situations where teachers are relatively free to pursue a line of development without the pressure of examinations or of syllabus. For example, a group of fifteen-year-olds at a Further Education College began with F4, 'National Characteristics'. They became involved with the idea of 'taking things for granted', so their teacher took them on to F2, 'Man's job/woman's work', F3, 'Tags for people', and D7, 'Expecting the usual'. Similarly a group of sixteen-year-olds with a very low level of literacy became intrigued by G1, 'Telling the tale', and moved on to A3, 'Judging your audience', and H3, 'Playing many parts', developing the theme of 'The same, only different'.

Finally, many teachers have used a unit or a group of units as a link between parts of a theme or between different activities. For example, a teacher exploring the theme of 'Teenagers' used J2, 'How adults see teenagers', to move away from a discussion of teenage problems towards a consideration of how some of these problems arise from the view which adults form of young people. In another situation, a teacher used C6, 'Intonation', to lead from a theme based on a study of 'Sound and symbol' into the new activity of play reading.

The comment of many teachers on the use of the units in this way was that they appreciated having the framework which the units gave to the theme, because they could be set on one side in the event of other options opening up without the feeling that the whole enterprise would come to nothing.

## 21 Can the units help with 'reluctant' learners?

They're good kids but they find most things beyond them.

They have to do English, but they're totally disinterested in anything I want to do with them.

They can read, just, but they won't write, and drama or poetry is just not on.

The three comments which head this section will, I hope, indicate what I mean by using the term 'reluctant'. It seemed to me to be the only term appropriate to cover a wide range of pupils, who for many and complex reasons present some intractable problems to the teacher of English. The three comments were made, respectively, by a primary teacher working with ten-year-olds whose IQ's ranged from 70 to 114, a young teacher taking English with electrical engineers on a Day Release course, and the Head of Department of a big comprehensive school where the fifth, sixth and seventh streams in the fourth year were rejecting almost everything his staff tried to offer. In the first case, the ability of the pupils was indeed a significant factor as they came from a socially and economically very deprived background. In the second group, ability was generally fairly high, but this was outweighed by the hostility generated in a situation where twenty-year-olds had come prepared to learn about electrical subjects and found they were also required to do 'English'. In the third group, ability was mixed, and hostility was rather less a factor than boredom with something which did not seem relevant to any of their own concerns. In all three cases, the teachers were willing to try using units, because they felt that 'anything was worth trying'. In the event, all three teachers felt that they had made some progress and the three examples given below will enable the reader to see in what way the units were able to contribute to the total situation.

There were twenty-four pupils in the first class, the seventh stream down in a very large middle school, and the proportion of low ability pupils in the group was high. The teacher decided to try unit B9, 'Advertising', and encouraged the pupils to bring in advertisements from newspapers or copy them down from television. Only four of the more able pupils brought in advertisements and no one offered anything written down from television. The teacher herself supplied a random selection of advertisements to each group of four children and asked them to pick out any advertisement in which they thought the wording was clever. They chose a Heinz baby food advertisement, 'The happiest beginners begin with Heinz' and a Tibs advertisement claiming to give a cat soft fur. They decided that these were clever advertisements, because mothers wanted babies to be happy so that they would not cry at night; and that people wanted cats to be soft and cuddly, so they would buy the appropriate products. The class also pointed out the double meaning of 'put a little in the kitty today'. Using this discussion as a point of departure, the teacher encouraged the children to go on and think about where advertisements of different kinds appear. They saw that the talcum powder and baby food advertisements would appear in women's magazines, while advertisements for fishing reels would appear in men's magazines and consequently would be very differently worded. They were also able to describe suitable advertisements for a fishing reel and a motor car and after a good deal of patient questioning the teacher drew the words 'technical language' from them. This led the class to suggesting a number of mechanical words and they were able to formulate the distinction between the language needed to advertise a Rolls-Royce as opposed to a family Ford car. One boy described the language which would be necessary for describing the Rolls-Royce as 'posh', another as 'pouffie'. At this point, the teacher produced plain paper and a list of subjects including a red duster, a cat or dog food, a special dress, a pan scrubber, a battery-powered bicycle and a waste bin. She asked the class to produce advertisements of their own. At the end of this session every pupil had produced an advertisement and many of them had shown considerable ingenuity:

Your rubbish is special rubbish it needs a gold-plated wastepaper bin—the present for the woman who has everything.

93

The electric bicycle, handy, safe, and educational: let your children learn to ride the electric way.

When the teacher completed the work she was not entirely satisfied with what had been done. She felt that the content of the advertisements the children had produced was not very high, but she later reported that she felt the children had gained from the discussion and were certainly more aware of the power of language as an advertising medium. What was even more exciting, however, only emerged a day or two later. Four boys of very low ability, who usually shrank from producing any written work at all, were so motivated that all they wanted to do was to write another advertisement! One of these boys, Richard, a boy with an IQ of 78, had produced the following:

This red duster will wipe grease and oil away from your motorbike.

This was a very encouraging effort when the report which accompanied this boy from his previous school had said, 'It is impossible to motivate Richard in order to produce work of any kind'.

A similar sort of comment might well have been made of the group of electrical engineers a young teacher in South-West England met in his classroom in a Further Education college some years ago. This time, however, ability was not the main problem. The group was mixed in ability, fairly lively, but easily distracted, and it would have been fatal, the teacher reported, to try to keep them sitting in desks for the whole three hours which the timetable assigned to 'English'. The situation was made rather more difficult by the fact that their previous teacher had not asked for *any* written work in the previous year, and there was a clamour of amazement when it was suggested that written work might be worth doing.

Against this background, a group of units was used, H5, 'Keeping up appearances', H10, 'Taking a hint', F9, 'Speaking "correctly"', E3, 'Reticence'. These units were chosen, partly because of the teacher's own interest in what he calls 'social abrasions', situations where the protective tissue, the rituals and observances that people use to make life safer and more reassuring for themselves, are scraped away, and partly because the group had been involved in a number of visits in the early part of the term, visits which included a mental health centre, the local assizes and a local cider factory, all of which were settings that would provide evidence about the way people use language to create or maintain 'front' and how others use language to break it down. In the event, the interest of the apprentices was engaged. E3, 'Reticence', initially gave them the chance 'to have a

94

bonanza on sex', but after a very short time they became involved in what was being said about the paradox between public and private faces, and they *offered* to write, subsequently producing interesting and insightful work which drew both on their own previous experience and on their recent experience of the visits. Several of the apprentices wrote amusingly, and at length, of the contrast between the public image of a judge and his private attempts to extricate himself from a compromising situation like being booked for parking, or encountering an old acquaintance whom he preferred to forget. Some wrote with understanding on the way language steers us clear of difficult areas, like the necessary self-protections which people need when dealing closely with death, for example the way hospital staff talk about 'stiffs' instead of 'corpses' or 'cadavers'. Others produced as much as two sides of foolscap, giving three or four dramatic incidents which exemplified different language styles. What did seem to come through all the work was a sense of enjoyment and achievement, which was all the more significant in that it was 'admitted', something which students of this kind often refuse to do. Commenting on his own work with the units and that of a colleague who taught in an Approved School, now a Community Home, this teacher wrote to us saying:

> I don't know how much feedback you get from teachers in Further Education, but my feeling is that *Language in Use* is almost unique in providing ways of interesting students who are often written off as recalcitrant, hostile or plain unteachable.

It would not be fair to say that the pupils in our final example, those in the comprehensive school I spoke of earlier, were recalcitrant, hostile or unteachable. It would be true to say that most of them were bored or disinterested while some, a minority, were voluble in condemning all activities involving poetry or drama. The teacher working with one of the groups chose E4, 'Half, please', because she hoped it would catch their interest, and because it seemed to relate directly to everyday life. The group of girls she was working with were girls of fifteen doing a 'homemaker's course' based on domestic science and art and craft. The girls were amenable, and not unfriendly, but they considered English 'a waste of time', irrelevant to their more practical activities. Against this fairly daunting background, the first session of 'Half, please' was quite promising.

In this session the class were presented with a number of very brief utterances, all out of context, and they were asked to supply the context using only the utterance given. This intrigued the class and

95

the single utterance 'Black or white?' produced fifteen possible contexts. These ranged from the easily predictable, such as a waiter asking a diner what sort of coffee he prefers, or a shop assistant asking a customer which colour gloves/shoes/underwear she prefers to the less familiar 'black or white', the respective sides of a sole which has to be skinned before cooking, i.e., 'black (side first) or white (side first)?'. Other 'blacks and whites', were related to colour schemes, distinctive markings (white ribbons on a wedding car, black for a funeral), football teams and racial discrimination. Some of the other utterances used, like 'Mr Speaker, sir', or 'Hymn number 20', had a more limited context. The class were quick to point out that some utterances, like 'Hymn 20', could only occur in a few particular settings, but others like 'black and white' could occur in very many settings and that, with this kind of phrase, 'You would know what it meant if you were there'. The teacher was somewhat uneasy about following the suggestion of the unit that the groups should write short dialogues to show how meanings can remain ambiguous for a long time if one relies upon the words alone to make sense of what is being said, because of the resistance of this group to anything which could be classified even loosely as 'drama', i.e., doing anything in front of the class. She did risk it, however, because the level of interest seemed so high. Fortunately, the ensuing improvisation went very well indeed. It was, in fact, successful enough to encourage the teacher to go on to unit E6, 'Colour labels', and then to unit A8, 'Words and diagrams', where the girls actually said that having worked through the unit they now felt much more confident with dress patterns and with operating instructions than they had ever been before. For the teacher, the units had been successful, in that, after a period in which she had failed to engage the class in anything she wanted to do, she now had a much better relationship with them and they felt that they had gained something from their work. Using the new relationship as a basis, the teacher was able to move to units where she had an opportunity to introduce plays, books and poems as illustrative material and in this way some progress was made in breaking down the girls' basic resistance towards literature. This they had derived from the attitudes of their own community and had preserved unmodified through all their years in school.

The three examples which I have sketched so briefly in this final section have focused on the fact that teachers of English very often have to operate in situations where what they want to do is limited by the existing attitudes of the pupils or students they teach. At times like these, a teacher has some difficult decisions to make and what I have tried to do in this section is to show what part the units can play in making these decisions, modifications or compromises. If a teacher is willing to adapt them to the situation he finds himself in, they will give him the chance to mobilise his pupils' experience of using language as ordinary people. This is something pupils cannot resist using, if they are given the opportunity. The involvement which comes out of this free use of their common experience of language and the world becomes in its turn the basis for all kinds of work which would otherwise be unthinkable.

# VI  Units across the curriculum

## 22  *Language in Use* and subject teachers—the problems

What has language got to do with teaching Geography?

What's a geographer doing at a Conference about language?

As he reads these two quotations, I would like the reader to replace the words 'Geography' and 'geographer' by the words that fit his own subject. Many subject teachers have used *Language in Use* successfully in the context of their own classrooms, but they have reported to us that they found themselves faced by a number of initial difficulties, difficulties which were quite unrelated to their own capabilities as teachers, to the design of the units, or to any particular aspect of the subjects themselves. It seems best, therefore, to begin this account of how the units can be related to subjects other than 'English' by looking at these difficulties.

Let me begin by asking a question of my own: what view of language in teaching and learning do these two quotations reveal? When I was first asked the question, 'What has language got to do with teaching Geography?', it did not seem like a question at all. On that occasion, the questioner did not expect, or want an answer. What the 'question' really implied was that the speaker could see no proper reason for a geographer being concerned about language. In her view, a geographer had a clearly defined responsibility, and that was to teach what was recognisably 'geographical'. What 'language' entered into the process, therefore, could not be the geographer's concern. I would go so far as to say that the remark was really a rebuke, a polite indication that I should restrict my attention to what was properly 'within my own field', and therefore, what I was *qualified* to discuss.

This idea of going outside 'one's own field' has a very direct bearing upon *Language in Use* and the subject teacher. If a subject teacher sees 'language' as being 'outside his field', because 'language' is 'English' and 'English' is a subject with its own responsibilities, just like his own, then it is highly likely that he will never even pick up *Language in Use* to see what it might have to offer him. He is likely to feel that he is trespassing upon territory that he has no right to enter, because it belongs legitimately only to those of his colleagues who are *qualified* to teach it, the 'English' specialists. On the other hand, if a subject specialist *does* appreciate the fact that the language he uses to teach his subject makes a particular kind of demand on his pupils, and is therefore as much a part of his professional concern as the organisation and presentation of the subject matter which he teaches, then he might pick up the units in all good faith and then run into a different set of problems. For example, if he begins to experiment with the units in the kind of school where strict boundaries are maintained between subjects, he may well find that 'language' is *done* by the English Department, who regard his efforts with the units merely as interference. More difficult still, his efforts to remedy his own language problems may be taken as a direct criticism of the English Department's work! For many subject specialists, therefore, strict boundaries between subjects may be what most deters them from using the units, or what creates a teaching situation in which they believe they can safely leave 'language' to the efforts of the English Department alone. The corollary of this is that, where they do, and their pupils fail to meet the linguistic demands the subject makes upon them, the English Department alone is blamed for this state of affairs.

In this section, therefore, I must make clear why I regard this state of affairs as unfair to teachers of English, subject teachers, and, most of all, to the pupils themselves. If everyone acts as if 'language' *is* 'English' and therefore can only be dealt with as a 'subject' in 'English' classes then ultimately it is the pupil who suffers most.

Let me put this crucial issue on one side for a moment, however, and take up the second of my two quotations, 'What's a geographer doing at a Conference about language?'. I was first asked this question by a Teacher/Adviser for English who had been trying to encourage teachers in his area to see that pupils *do* have language needs in *every* classroom. Unlike my first questioner, this teacher really did want an answer to his question, because his wide experience in schools had already convinced him that language *had to be* the concern of *all* teachers. He wanted to know how I had come to the same conclusion as he had, working from within one subject only in the curriculum. I found it difficult to explain to him how I had arrived at the idea that my pupils' 'failure' was often caused by the language difficulties which they faced, and not by their inability to grasp the concepts I presented to them. My difficulty was precisely the difficulty pupils themselves frequently experience in the subject classroom, the difficulty of putting into words for another person something which you have not completely grasped yourself and have never before attempted to verbalise. Unlike many pupils, however, I had three things to help me, a listener who really *wanted* to hear my answer, the freedom to select my own way of organising my thoughts and the freedom to use *words of my own choosing*. Eventually, what I did was to describe to him the one incident which, more than any other, had alerted me to the complexity of the problems I and my pupils faced in finding and using a common language for teaching and learning.

The fourth year had been working on glaciation. I had begun the topic in my usual way by showing them my colour slides of glacial features, both exotic examples, like the Alps and the Svartisen glacier, and local pictures, like the Mournes and the Glens of Antrim. I drew diagrams, produced models and talked about them. I took great care that the class was not put off by the very large number of technical terms which I needed to use, terms like 'corrie', 'arête', 'horn', 'moraine', 'erratic', 'striations', 'hanging valley' and 'drumlin'. We spent a day on fieldwork in the Mournes where we looked at many of the features, sketched them, photographed them and walked over them. All seemed to be going well. Back in school, I then decided to complete the work by using an idea I had developed from the unit 'Judging your audience', a unit which I had used successfully by then with many different groups throughout the school. I asked my fourth form to work in groups. Each group was to prepare two reports on their glaciation work, one for me and one for the second form, who had not as yet done any work on glaciation. I hoped that the report for the second form audience would develop my fourth-formers' awareness of the new terms they had met, because they would have to make use of them in the report and find out how to explain their meaning to readers who would not be able to bring to their reading any prior knowledge of the terms. Using the unit framework, however, meant that the fourth-formers would be free to organise both their thoughts and their language in any way they chose, so long as the result met the requirements of their audience. The work went forward very well and the finished reports were presented to the second-formers in a joint session. The second-formers were eager to do their part and they were asked how much of the reports they could understand without difficulty as this would give the fourth form a real measure of the success with which they had been able to judge and meet the needs of their audience. I was myself pleased with the quality of the written work and the ease with which the fourth-formers were handling the fairly formidable technical language of the topic.

100

After the second-formers had left, the fourth form talked over with me the results of their efforts: they agreed that explaining something to someone else, who had not, as yet, met the concepts you needed to use, was a very difficult task. They thought it would have been virtually impossible for them if they had not been able to use the diagrams they had drawn and the pictures they had taken during their fieldtrip. What they said was so interesting that I asked them if they would put their comments down on paper for me, concentrating on any difficulties they had experienced or observed in the joint session with the second form. They did this for 'geography homework' and two days later, by my own fireside, I came across the following comment:

> The second-formers did not have as much difficulty as I thought they would. They found 'terms' easy to understand, because these were explained, but they had trouble with ordinary words. One girl asked me what a boulder was and I didn't know, and no one in our group really knew, so I had to ask people in the other groups till I found out. . . .

Like the teacher who could not remember what E.R.N.I.E. stood for, this was the moment when I wished that I had never heard of *Language in Use*, for what it had done was show me that I had never thought of explaining a 'simple' common language word like 'boulder'. I had taken it for granted that *everyone* would know what a boulder was. Had it not been for the informal situation, a situation in which the girls were able to discover what they did *not* know, then their ignorance of the meaning of the word 'boulder' would have remained undiscovered despite my pleas to 'make sure you ask if I ever use a word that you don't understand'. When I told this story to a Physics teacher who had had considerable experience in the middle levels of a large girls' comprehensive school in London, she responded by saying that she had met a strong parallel case in her own teaching. She thought that many girls were put off Physics, or discouraged, because Physics habitually used common language words like 'gear', 'pulley', 'billiard ball', 'projectile', 'dynamo' in its descriptions and these words belong essentially to the world of boys' experience. She pointed out that many of the metaphors, analogies and examples used in textbooks are drawn from cars, motor cycles, guns and rockets, and these are all matters which lie outside the common experience of very many girls. They have been successfully deterred from acquiring any real experience of them because the common culture has taught them that these matters are properly masculine matters, and must be left to their brothers to explore.

101

The implications of both these examples seem clear to me. No matter how sympathetic I had been towards the language difficulties of my pupils, and no matter how aware of my pupils' needs I had thought myself to be, I was not able to do anything actively, simply by being aware of the problem myself, for I could hardly expect pupils to tell me what their difficulties were when they themselves were not aware of them. Once I was aware that there might be difficulties, I had to go on and find ways of revealing these difficulties to my pupils themselves by creating situations in which they would carry on with their geographical work, but, at the same time, be free to organise their thoughts in *language of their own choosing* to meet the specific needs of the task before them. Through these situations, they would be able to discover the points at which the language they wanted to use presented problems for them. By discovering this for themselves in a free working situation, the problems could be accepted and resolved without the shadow of 'being wrong' or 'not knowing the answer'. In my case, it was fortunate that this decision on my part had grown from my work with the units, for it was a further use of the units that helped me to continue to explore these difficulties as they occurred in my own subject, and subsequently, with the aid of six of my colleagues, as I shall describe in the next section, explore them in other subjects also.

Let us think for a moment of one very likely reaction to the 'boulder' story. 'Imagine not knowing what a boulder was, how incredible!' But is it incredible? Is there any reason why words known to one person need be known to another *unless* both have had a common experience of the contexts from which those words take their meaning, be they the contexts of thought or action? Why should a fourteen-year-old town dweller's experience particularly include the word 'boulder'? Is it really a common language word that she is likely to hear regularly on the lips of those about her or use herself in talking about her everyday experience? Need she have read stories set in wild country; or, even if she had, need she be presumed to have stopped her reading to look it up in a dictionary; and if she had, what *sense* would she have then been able to make of what the dictionary told her? So, is it any reflection on this fourteen-year-old's ability and intelligence, if she has somehow managed to miss out on the word 'boulder'? Is not the fact that she had just grasped, and been able to explain, the much more esoteric physical features such as 'corrie' and 'moraine' a better measure of her capabilities than her ignorance of 'boulder'?

One of the problems we subject specialists have is that we have lived with our chosen subject for so long that its concepts, its technical terms, and its ways of speaking are all so well known to us and so fluently used, that they seem second nature to us. It is difficult for us to recall a time when 'evaporation' or 'kinetic energy' or 'feudalism' or 'bathos' or 'vector' or 'osmosis' or 'perspective' or 'octave' was a word which other people used accurately and fluently but which we did not ourselves fully grasp. However much we might wish it were not so, there is no simple way of 'putting out of mind', even temporarily, our cumulative experience of the concepts, and the language, which make up our knowledge of our particular subject in order to put ourselves in the position of our pupils when they meet this language for the first time. Language once learnt so enters our experience that we cannot 'forget' the way we have come to see the world with its help. In this sense, language is a one-way process of change. Only something as destructive as injury to the brain, or the process of 'brainwashing', can eradicate the effects of the way we learn language through experience of thought or action.

What we *can* do, however, is to create in our classrooms the conditions in which our pupils can learn the language and the concepts which subject work requires by the same process that they have already used to learn the language and the concepts which inform their lives as members of family, community and society. How we can do this, I take up in the next section, because I must now explain what I meant when I said earlier that it is unfair to teachers of English, to other subject teachers, and most of all to pupils, to think that 'language' is 'English' and therefore need only come up for particular consideration in the context of 'English' class.

It is not surprising that we do have difficulty, when we use the same name to mean two things at once, the language and the subject. It is certainly true that the pupil's use of spoken and written English is properly a central concern of the 'English' specialist, but the 'English' specialist does not usually see himself as the person who can teach a pupil how to write a history essay or spell the word 'molecule'. He does, indeed, have a special relationship to English, because he is the person who must accept the basic responsibility for the mother tongue, both in speaking and in writing. He must help pupils develop a basic confidence and fluency in their use of spoken and written language, but he is *not* in a position to teach them the whole range of language for learning the curriculum demands from them. The language needed for learning, and help with the necessary ways of using it, must be provided for pupils in the context of the laboratory or the workshop, the mathematics room or the

103

history room, the art room or the modern languages room, itself. They can learn the ways of speaking and writing which they need only in the actual context of the work they are asked to do, because their *experience* of the problems the work presents is crucial to their discovery of the appropriate ways of formulating them in words. It is interesting to see that the physicist, quoted on page 101, had come to very much the same conclusions as myself after my work with my geographers. The possession of whatever confidence and fluency the English Department can develop for them is not, *by itself*, going to give pupils the language they need for their work across the whole range of the curriculum.

However important the contribution of the English Department to the subject specialist's task, it is the subject specialist, and he alone, who must accept final responsibility for meeting the language needs which he himself creates.

## 23 *Language in Use* and subject specialists—the possibilities

The path to *Language in Use* may indeed be fraught with difficulties for many subject teachers, but it does seem that more and more subject specialists are prepared to face them. In the three years since the first publication of *Language in Use* much has occurred to make the situation easier: the reorganisation of many schools; new publications about teaching and learning; the introduction of mixed ability classes and team teaching; the growth of integrated studies and changes in the traditional boundaries of the curriculum such as the coming of RoSLA has promoted; all these have led to an easing of rigid boundaries between subjects and a climate in which problems can now be shared. Whatever the reasons, many subject teachers are now using the units to tackle their own language problems in the context of their own classrooms.

What I want to do in this section, therefore, is to describe how one small group of subject specialists, of which I was a member, started to work with the units. Then I shall go on to comment on the work of other specialists whose work I have since come to know of.

The work with the units in my school began, more or less where I began this book, at the point where I used my first unit from the trial version, 'Writing for an audience', now 'Judging your audience'. It seemed to me that this unit was relevant to any situation in which pupils were required to use language in a way sharply constrained by the needs of the situation, and I asked a number of my colleagues if they would help me to test out this thought. When we met together we comprised a biologist, a chemist, a historian, two domestic scientists, an R.E. specialist and myself, a geographer. Our first meeting was a significant one for we realised that it was the first occasion that any group of teachers in the school had met together to exchange ideas about their mutual *teaching* problems. What emerged in those first meetings was that many of our problems in classrooms *were the same and not different*. Up to this point we had seen our problems as the problems of *subject* teachers, and therefore problems which must be essentially quite different each from the other, because the subject matter we were dealing with was so very different. What emerged from our discussion of my work with 'Judging your audience' was that all six subjects represented at our discussions required pupils to write with a similar focus on a specific 'audience', something which initially, or even subsequently, they could not do; and that we *all* required pupils to use language in specific ways to solve the specific problems our work presented to them, which again, initially they were unable to do successfully. The point was put most clearly when one of the domestic science teachers said:

> It seems to me that setting in a sleeve is not so different as I thought from cutting up a dogfish or doing an experiment. In each of them, you have to be able to follow instructions: and in each, presumably, you have to be able to give some account of what you have done?

The biologist and chemist accepted that this indeed was the case and as a result we all went away to think about the possibility of using a version of 'Judging your audience' to tackle a specific problem of this kind as it arose in our own classrooms.

The chemist and the biologist worked together. One result of their efforts I have used already in Section 13, page 54, to illustrate the reasons for the use of particular ways of working in the units. The reader will remember that what they did was to ask a group of girls who had been absent to carry out and record a particular experiment, using only the notebooks of the girls who had already done it. The result of the work was to show the whole class why the writing up of an experiment required so methodical an organisation and so careful and precise a use of language.

The two domestic science teachers used the unit with a class of very demoralised fifth-formers who claimed that 'they didn't know anything because they were the B's'; and that they 'couldn't write because we get bad marks for English'. The domestic science teachers set these girls the task of writing instructions which would show first-year pupils how to set in a sleeve and how to bake an apple-tart. Many of their experiences during the work were paralleled by my own experiences with the sixth-formers who wrote about 'pollution', because the fifth-formers also met the problem of how to treat technical terms like, 'tuck' or 'knead', or instructions like, 'Grease an 8″ tin', if you are writing for people who do not know how 'to tuck' or 'to grease', because they have not, as yet, had the chance to experience these activities. The domestic science teachers were pleased with what was done on paper but even more pleased by the spin-off from the work. In writing for first-formers, the fifth-formers became aware of the number of technical terms and instructions which they could cope with quite competently. What the unit had done was to focus their attention on what they *knew*, rather than what they did not know, and the result was a significant rise in their confidence and a much happier approach towards their work. The sharing of the work also enabled the teachers themselves to develop a whole new range of ways of describing and commenting on pupils' work, because the experience they had shared they could apply to other situations. Both teachers felt that the rise in confidence of their pupils, and the increased understanding of the problems of technical language, more than justified the time they had spent on the unit, even had the writing itself not been as good as it turned out to be.

Working with a small group of able A-level students, the historian was not as concerned about their writing as she was about their assessment of the historical evidence with which they were presented, both in textbooks and in the facsimile reproductions of original and contemporary writings. She adapted 'Judging your audience' as follows. On the occasion of a major debate, preceding a vote of confidence in the Prime Minister of Northern Ireland (March 1970), she obtained a copy of Hansard for the Northern Ireland House of Parliament. On the following day, she bought a selection of newspapers, both English national newspapers like *The Times* and the *Daily Mail*, and Irish national papers like *The Irish Times* and specifically Ulster papers like *The Belfast Telegraph*, and the *Newsletter*. What she then asked her class to do was to work in small groups, outlining in colour all the references to the debate in all the newspapers, and then to compare what was said in each newspaper report with the copy of Hansard which provided a word-by-word record of what was actually said in the debate. What the class discovered was the wide degree of difference possible in the reporting of 'the facts' about the same event, when reports were written for very different audiences. The historian also considered the question of bias and of the comparative proportions of 'reporting', 'commentating' and 'speculating' which the various newspapers considered appropriate for their audiences. From their discussion of their findings, the pupils worked out the idea that what they imagined teachers wanted to see in their written work might not fit at all with what teachers actually looked to see.

As a result of this conclusion, the class decided to find out just what the staff did mean when they used the word 'essay' to indicate the kind of work they wanted. First, they made their own 'predictions' about what individual members of staff might be asking for when they set an 'essay'. Then the girls designed a questionnaire in the form of a grid with features like 'accurate reporting', 'presentation of facts', 'commenting', 'précis of information previously given', 'description', and asked each member of staff to tick those features she had in mind when she set an 'essay'. What they discovered was that there were very wide variations in the combination of features individual members of staff selected; and that a pupil could be faced with meeting as many as seven quite different combinations of features within the spectrum of the staff who taught her at any one time, and all called by the one name 'essay'.

The girls then turned to compare the completed questionnaires with the 'predictions' which they themselves had made. They found that where their own A-level subjects were concerned, there was a high degree of correlation between a teacher's expectations and their own prediction, but where they had made their prediction from their experience of O-level subjects, or subjects which they had dropped at an early stage in their career, there were serious discrepancies. The idea of using a modified form of this questionnaire to help younger children find out what staff were really asking for was something which the seven of us considered in our further group discussions.

The teacher of religious education had finally decided that she did not want to use 'Judging your audience' at this point in her work because she did not see a way of fitting it to her existing programme. She had taken away *Language in Use*, however, and had looked at unit D13, 'Preaching', which she decided to try with a 'rather difficult' group of 'C' stream girls whose attention she found it extremely difficult to hold for any length of time. The *Language in Use* tape, which provides an example of a sermon was not then available, but this teacher hit on the idea of using a quite different resource. She took the sermon from *Beyond the Fringe*, a comedy review of the 1960s, which was available on an LP record of the show.

In it, a sermon is preached on the text, 'But my brother Esau is an hairy man, but I, *I* am a smooth man'. From the point of view of presentation and use of language she considered it devastatingly accurate, and for people like her pupils, who had considerable experience of dull or wordy or unenlightening sermons, she considered it would be very, very funny. The results were indeed illuminating. Not only were her pupils intrigued and amused to such an extent that their attention never wandered, but they showed a quite unprecedented willingness to participate in the ensuing discussion. More surprisingly still was the speed with which the class moved towards important issues in their talk. They asked themselves whether or not the sermon would offend people; whether it was right to 'make fun of' ways of speaking which were out of date or meaningless to most of their intended audience; and whether or not sermons should be delivered in a 'normal' voice in 'normal' language. This led her to suggest that they look at more examples. They made use of BBC five-minute sermons and parts of addresses from interdenominational services. They also made recordings of the school assembly. In each case, they looked at the ways in which 'preaching' is modified by the context in which it occurs. Her report to the group was that she had more serious discussion of the topics which were her immediate specialist concern by using the unit than she had had throughout her previous year's work with the group using methods of a more orthodox kind.

Perhaps the group of subject specialists who have most quickly seen the potential of the units have been those working with practical or scientific subjects such as Physics, Chemistry, Biology, Domestic Science, Woodwork or Craft. They have made especial use of those units which focus upon the relationship between actions and words. Starting with a unit like A1 which sets out:

> to show that the description of the sequence of events involved in even a simple homely task like tying a shoe lace can put a great strain upon an individual's command of the language, because language in itself is not well-fitted to descriptions of this kind,

they have worked through those units which they feel will best make both them and their pupils aware of where the difficulties lie. One physicist suggests that this unit is very useful if it is used in combination with the 'Introductory Circus' from the first year of the Nuffield Combined Science course. The idea is that many different objects are left out around the laboratory, items such as springs, polystyrene balls, plastic rulers, rubber bands and so on. A1 provides an excellent

108

framework within which the teacher can ask questions like, 'What *exactly* does happen when you pull a spring and then let go?'. Other scientists report that they have found A7, 'Operating instructions', A8, 'Words and diagrams', A9, 'New words' and A10, 'Observing and describing', particularly helpful. Moreover, they have found that one unit is capable of a very general application, F7, 'Weather forecasting'. It can be modified to explore the relationship between the scientific view of any set of facts and the way we customarily think about those facts as a result of the language we use to talk about them in the course of our everyday experience.

One scientist we have talked to argues that all science courses should begin by working units G8, 'Technical terms' and G10, 'Writing up', so that teacher and pupil can then 'get on with the job'. These units would, indeed, be useful, worked into the early stages of a course, but there is real danger in the idea that you can somehow do your language first and then get on with the job. Language for learning, and for teaching, remains an inescapable part of that job. As another scientist put it:

> No pupil can be expected to battle with difficult new language if he is not stimulated and feels the need for that new language. The pupil *must* do the experiment himself—please, no class demonstrations—and then *need* the language to convey what has happened. If they have been encouraged and stimulated, most pupils will want to tell others what has happened in their experiments and it is at this point, when he is struggling to find words for what he *wants* to convey, that you give him the necessary terms.

However, our first scientist had certainly thought his way beyond the position of a third scientist who, at a recent Conference in Manchester, proposed that science teaching be abandoned in favour of extra English lessons, until such time as pupils had mastered the necessary language for writing up a 'simple' experiment and the ability to understand a set of 'simple' instructions.

For mathematicians, a critical unit appears to be A8, 'Words and diagrams'. Of all the subject specialists across the curriculum, it is often the mathematician who is most sceptical of the need for any work to do with language within his own orbit. He is inclined to reply that Mathematics has its own language and that is his proper concern. In the light of this common response, it is interesting to see the way in which specific reference to language is built into the programme of one Mathematics course, designed to cover the needs of pupils from nursery age to the early secondary stage, called 'Guidelines', and

109

prepared by the Mathematics Department of the Manchester College of Education. In the introduction itself, the team states that 'Children are encouraged to study in depth, *asking their own questions and finding their own answers*' (my italics). They then go on to comment in this way on the origins of 'Guidelines':

> The idea of making a chart such as *Guidelines* grew out of departmental discussions about organising schemes for the teaching of mathematics. The difficulties we sometimes had during these discussions in understanding what others meant by their captions brought home to us the need for writing the notes.

It seems that even very experienced teachers of Mathematics, working within as precise a field of operations as mathematics, can find that there is a problem of *linguistic* meaning confronting them. How much more so, therefore, is this likely to be the case for the pupil?

In the actual programmes of work, the initial item under a specific heading like 'Time', or 'Sets' or 'Number and operation' is an explicit reference to use of the appropriate language. The actual wording in this last case is:

N1   Use of language for sorting and ordering.

What the design of the course implies is that a pupil learning mathematics has to move from talking about the relevant relationships in the common language of experience to using the abstract formulation of the language of mathematics for representing them. Success with the latter, therefore, depends upon the pupil being able to maintain the link between the real events of his experience and the way they can be represented in the abstract language of mathematics. Retaining his ability to *talk about* the link between the two is crucial to his being able to maintain it. When Professor Christopher Zeeman was being interviewed about his new Mathematics Institute at the University of Warwick some years ago, he said that one of the chief objects of the Institute was 'to have lots of talking' between the visiting mathematicians, because '. . . you can convey most about new things talking face-to-face'. The interviewer challenged this, along the lines of our sceptical mathematician's objections to working with language in his own environment, by saying that he thought mathematics was about numbers and symbols. Professor Zeeman's reply was this:

> Oh yes, of course. But you can't *talk* in numbers and symbols. If you can't talk about numbers and symbols, you'll never have the right intuitions to do mathematics successfully.

110

On the much less exalted level of the ordinary secondary school mathematics class, the same would seem to hold true.

With geographers, and teachers of social studies or history, the units grouped in Part III: 'Language and social man', have been the most frequently used. The exploration of how society works can be approached locally by considering the school as a society, using units K1, 'Schools and colleges' and K2, 'School traditions', while J1, 'Belonging to a group', and J2, 'How adults see teenagers', can help pupils to explore the ways in which individual human groups create and maintain their identity. K3, 'Negotiating', has been much used by historians who want to demonstrate the difficulties of what we call 'democratic processes'. The units from 'Language and Culture,' units F1 to F11, have enabled both geographers and historians to explore the differences between social groups who do not share a common culture. It would seem that F2, 'Man's job/woman's work,' is one of the most frequently used units in the whole volume, focusing as it does on the way the words of our language can perpetuate ideas and assumptions.

One short section cannot be a 'Complete Guide to the use of units across the curriculum'. That must wait upon the time when many more subject specialists have worked with the units and thought through the implications for their use in their particular area of the curriculum. What I hope I have been able to do is to suggest that the units do contain an immense potential which is available to every teacher, whatever his subject, to explore and then exploit, for himself in the light of his own problems and practice.

# Postscript

Having come with us so far, readers may well ask, 'What next?'. Firstly, we would not pretend that we have been able to answer every question about working with language. There are two reasons for this. To be really useful, a book of this kind must have limits. Time is very precious to all teachers and a bulky tome is not a welcoming prospect, whatever the potential value of its content. For this reason, we have taken up only those questions which relate to the initial stages of working with language. Certainly, each chapter could be extended to the length of a book itself were we to follow out all the implications of the issues they raise. Moreover, were we to go much beyond the limits we have set ourselves we would have had to make use of many ideas about language and its use that would be unfamiliar to our readers. As it is perfectly possible to go a long way with work of this kind before an understanding of these ideas becomes essential, it seemed to us that we should carry the reader as far as we could without drawing upon them and include in the Postscript a small number of titles which would enable him to find out about them for himself when he chose.

Secondly, there is a very good reason why we cannot hope to answer all the questions teachers might ask, that is quite independent of any limitations of space or scope. It is a reason which arises out of the very nature of teaching itself. There is an important sense in which every teaching situation is unique: it is what this teacher does, with these pupils, of this age and ability and background, in this school, in this curriculum context, at this point in the school year. When any teacher attempts something new in the classroom, or presents old things in new ways, there will be questions that arise out of this immediate context. Now it is these questions a book of this kind, or any book for that matter, can only answer indirectly. Given a certain teaching situation it can point to what might be generally relevant in the circumstances but every teacher has to take what is said in general terms and relate it to his own classroom for himself, for there are basic decisions to be made which relate only to that teaching situation at that moment in time. No teacher can ask another to make these basic decisions for him, therefore, as they are necessarily bound up with the particular circumstances in which he finds himself. The most serious criticism to be made of certain kinds of so-called 'structured materials' for the classroom is that they deprive the teacher of the power to make these decisions. As the reader has discovered, it is a central feature of the units that each teacher needs to decide for himself how he can best use them in the circumstances of his own particular teaching situation. Consequently, questions will necessarily arise for him that no outsider could possibly predict with any certainty and provide answers to.

It is for this reason that we would suggest the need for collaboration with others as the most important next step for a teacher setting out to develop his work with language. Collaboration, first, within the context of the school itself. There is no better way to tease out the questions which arise from the immediate local teaching situation than to sit round the table with a number of colleagues who are making the same efforts to develop their work with language. As so many teachers have said to us, the simple act of having to make explicit the problem they have met is often enough *in itself* to show them the way to a possible solution. At the same time, there is great comfort and support to be had from hearing a colleague say, 'Yes, that was just my problem too and I tried this'. Many teachers have come to value *Language in Use* precisely because its use has created the need for this kind of discussion and thus helped to break down the limiting isolation of classroom or subject in which so many of them still find themselves.

This kind of discussion about the practical problems of implementing and developing successful work with language can very easily lead on to discussion of a language policy for the whole curriculum. Many teachers have said that their efforts can only go so far, because the approach to language they encourage within their own classrooms is contradicted by what pupils are faced with elsewhere. The more attention teachers pay to the part played by language in the work of their own classroom the more pressing becomes the need for a common approach to language within the school. Such a common approach, however, does need to grow out of the exploration of mutual problems and the sharing of successful solutions. Attitudes to language are very personal things and an imposed policy can be worse than no policy at all in its effects upon the language climate of the school.

So far, we have suggested action within the school itself, but no school is an island. The school down the road may face similar problems and have found its way to a solution which could be readily adapted to one's own situation. Many of our visits to talk about *Language in Use* were to Teachers' Centres and it seems to us that there is no more valuable role that these centres can play than to provide the meeting place and the resources for teachers to form working groups in which they can explore and share experience from a wide diversity of teaching situations. In a new area like working with language, meeting together in this way provides much of the support and encouragement a teacher needs. Moreover, we have found that many teachers soon want to find out more about language and the part it plays in teaching and learning. The Teachers' Centre can then provide the courses and speakers and books they need.

Finding out more about language and how we use it for living and learning brings us at last to the question of what to read next. We want to suggest just a few titles which will carry the reader on to the next stage. The references to the relevant literature that they contain will then enable him to go wherever he wishes in his exploration of this field. As the reader will have discovered, the idea of 'language for living' is very much a part of the argument we have presented, and 'language for living' implies a very close relationship between the language we speak and the life we lead. This relationship we explore in our own book, *Language and Community*, a book written specifically for teachers. The idea of 'language for learning', on the other hand, leads to questions about the relationship between the pupil's experience of language and the school's attitudes to language and its use. *Language, Experience and School* explores the issues involved and gives a well illustrated account of how the school imposes its demands upon the pupil for particular ways of using language without always realising that this is what it is doing.

Both these titles belong to the new series of books called *Explorations in Language Study*. This series grew out of the *Language in Use* enterprise, for it was clear to all those concerned that the particular needs of teachers were very little catered for when it came to books about language and its use. So the idea of a field of enquiry that would focus upon the whole question of language in teaching and learning was developed, and given the name 'Language Study'. What 'Language Study' is, and why it needs to be taken seriously by everyone concerned with education, is the subject of *Language Study, the Teacher and the Learner*, which also contains a basic bibliography. These titles have been selected, both to show the relevance of many different subjects to the study of language in education, and to help the teacher who is likely to be unfamiliar with many of them.

We have stressed already the importance of what we might call the social and cultural aspect of 'language for living'. There is also what we might call the individual, or psychological aspect to be considered. Just as we use language to create a society and its culture,

114

so do we use language to create for ourselves an individual picture of the world that is personally meaningful to us. One of the most readable accounts of this complex process is James Britton's *Language and Learning*. As he is himself a thoughtful and sensitive teacher, with great experience of children and their learning, he is able to adopt a Language Study point of view, so that it is easy to relate what he says to the teaching situation.

Lastly, there is the question of language itself, its form and organisation, the idea of language as a coherent and rationally designed 'something' that we all possess, however incoherent and irrational our own use of it may at times appear. We want to suggest three titles here, each one different in character and approach, because this is a subject where the chosen approach of the author is directly reflected in the shape he gives to his presentation of 'language' and the approach that will suit one reader may well alienate another.

Two of them are by figures who were 'founding fathers' in the development of the scientific study of language in this century, and both were written for the layman, because their authors felt that what this new science of Linguistics was discovering was too important to remain locked up in the files of academic journals. The main purpose of *Language* by the American, Edward Sapir, is to show:

> what I conceive language to be, what is its variability in place and time, and what are its relations to other fundamental human interests—the problem of thought, the nature of the historical process, race, culture, art.

The character of *The Tongues of Men*, by the Englishman, Firth, is well shown in the following two quotations:

> . . . language can be regarded as operator, switchboard, and wiring in control of our social currents and power. It is the nervous system of our society . . .

> . . . speech is social 'magic' . . . the origins of speech must be sought in the way we all learn it and use it in the course of life.

Finally, there is *The Labyrinth of Language*, by another American, Max Black, a philosopher by trade who is also a very successful teacher of his subject. Once again, we will give two quotations to show the kind of approach to language the writer has adopted:

> Man is the only animal that can talk. More generally, he is the

only animal that can use *symbols* (words, pictures, graphs, numbers, etc.). He alone can bridge the gap between one person and another, conveying thoughts, feelings, desires, attitudes, and sharing in the traditions, conventions, the knowledge and the superstition of his culture; the only animal that can truly *understand* and *misunderstand*. On this essential skill depends everything that we call civilization. Without it, imagination, thought—even self-knowledge—are impossible.

Consequently:

To be deprived of speech is to lack the indispensable prerequisite for a human community.

Taken together, we hope that these seven books will provide the reader with a starting point for his own exploration of the questions about language and its use which his reading of this book, and his own attempts at language work in the classroom, have raised for him. It is now for the reader to choose the direction, the length and the scope of the journey he wishes to make through the territory of 'language study'.

## Books referred to in the Postscript

*Language and Community*, Anne and Peter Doughty, Edward Arnold, 1974.
*Language, Experience and School*, Geoffrey Thornton, Edward Arnold, 1974.
*Language Study, the Teacher and the Learner*, Peter Doughty and Geoffrey Thornton, Edward Arnold, 1973.
*Language and Learning*, James Britton, Penguin, 1972.
*Language*, Edward Sapir, Rupert Hart-Davis, 1963.
*The Tongues of Men*, J. R. Firth, Oxford University Press, 1964.
*The Labyrinth of Language*, Max Black, Penguin, 1972.

The titles marked * are all in the Edward Arnold series *Explorations in Language Study*, edited by Peter Doughty and Geoffrey Thornton. Other titles in this series include:

*Language in Bilingual Communities*, Derrick Sharp, 1973.
*Language in the Junior School*, Eric Ashworth, 1973.

For publication early in 1975:

*Accent, Dialect and the School*, Peter Trudgill.
*The World, the Child and his Language*, edited by Sinclair Rogers.

# Books referred to in the text

*Language in Use*, Doughty, Pearce and Thornton, Edward Arnold, 1971.
*Teaching as a Subversive Activity*, Neil Postman/Charles Weingartner, Penguin Education Special, 1971.
*The Foundations of Language*, Andrew Wilkinson, Oxford University Press, 1971.
*Exploring Language*, Doughty, Pearce and Thornton, Edward Arnold, 1972.
*Language, the learner and the school*, Barnes, Britton, Rosen and the L.A.T.E., Penguin Papers in Education, 1969 and 1971.
*The Language of Primary School Children*, Connie and Harold Rosen, Penguin Education, 1973.

# Appendix I

## I Language—its nature and function

### Using language to convey information

A1   Words and actions
A2   Reading and understanding
A3   Judging your audience
A4   Reporting events
A5*   Language and the Law
A6   Reporting Parliament
A7   Operating instructions
A8   Words and diagrams
A9   New words
A10*   Observing and describing
A11   Summarising
A12   Making an abstract
A13   Sports commentating

### Using language expressively

B1   Formal and informal
B2*   Making speeches
B3   Reading the News
B4   Notices
B5   Front page
B6   Bias
B7   Fact and fiction
B8   Persuasion
B9   Advertising

### Sound and symbol

C1*   Speech and writing
C2   Making a script
C3*   Distinctive voices
C4   Accent
C5*   What is speech?
C6   Intonation
C7   Implications
C8   Words and gestures
C9   Dialogue
C10   Spelling

### Pattern in language

D1   Sounds, words, and meaning
D2   Order in sentences
D3   Words in sequence
D4   Patterns in language
D5   What is a rule?
D6   What do we correct?
D7   Expecting the usual
D8   Marked and unmarked
D9   Names in the High Street
D10   What is 'difficult'?
D11   Meaning
D12   Ambiguity and ambivalence
D13*   Preaching

## II Language and individual man

### Language and reality

E1   Animal, vegetable, or mineral
E2   Birds and beasts
E3   Reticence
E4   Half, please
E5   Abstract, general, and particular
E6   Colour labels
E7   'Write me an essay'
E8   Fiction and reality
E9   Fiction and documentary

### Language and culture

F1   Nice/nasty
F2   Man's job/woman's work
F3   Tags for people
F4   National characteristics
F5   Attitudes from fiction
F6   The language of religion
F7   Weather forecasting
F8   How we use slang
F9   Speaking 'correctly'
F10   Regional speech
F11   How writers exploit regional speech

## Language and experience

G1 Telling the tale
G2★ Watching games
G3 Slanting the news
G4 Making predictions
G5 Making up questionnaires
G6 Catch phrases
G7 Writing the rules
G8 Technical terms
G9 The language of school subjects
G10 Writing up
G11 Praise and blame
G12 Reviewer and audience
G13 Language and art

# III Language and social man

## Language in individual relationships

H1 Family names
H2 Personal names
H3 Playing many parts
H4 Changing jobs
H5 Keeping up appearances
H6 Being natural
H7 Pub and club
H8 Keeping one's distance
H9 Being tactful
H10 Taking a hint

## Language in social relationships

J1 Belonging to a group
J2 How adults see teenagers
J3 Crowds
J4 Social talk
J5 What is conversation?
J6★ Conversation between friends
J7★ Family talk
J8 Being interviewed
J9 Interviews on television
J10 Talking on the telephone
J11 Taking messages

## Language in social organisations

K1 Schools and colleges
K2 School traditions
K3 Negotiating
K4 Applying for a job
K5 Starting work
K6 Communicating
K7 Letters
K8 Speech-making
K9 Projecting an image
K10 Informing the public
K11★ Reports from interviews

★ These units require use of a tape-recorder.

# Appendix II

## Judging your audience

This unit considers an aspect of language which is fundamental to writing: it must be directed towards a specific context if it is to convey the information successfully.

It explores the degree to which the writer's view of his audience must strongly determine his way of writing. When the object is to convey a body of information, this aspect of the writer's task is so important that the success of his efforts depends to a large extent on his success in judging the needs of the reader for whom he is writing.

---

[1] In this session, the class works out for each of three texts in turn its intended audience. It is best done with the class working in pairs or small groups. When they have done this, they should select a topic, well-known to them, and each write three pieces, each one for different audiences. The texts should be short, about 150 words in all, and the audiences well-differentiated. The following suggestions may be useful:

| | | |
|---|---|---|
| (a) feature in a mass daily | lead article in a Sunday Review | *New Society* |
| (b) Penguin Special | school text-book | academic article |
| (c) a review in mass daily | —in serious weekly | —in specialist journal |
| (d) record sleeve | *Melody Maker* | *The Gramophone* |

[2] This session uses the texts written by the class. These should be circulated and the class, working in pairs or in groups, should assess how successfully they meet the needs of the audiences for which they are intended. Points to look for include:

    (a) inappropriate use of technical language for the level of the audience chosen

    (b) assumption of too much or too little background knowledge in the reader

    (c) condescension towards a non-specialist reader

    (d) choice of a style which is too formal or too relaxed for the audience concerned.

3] Select a text intended for an educated adult reader, dealing with a topic in the area of a school subject like history or geography, and ask the class to re-write it for eleven-year-olds. Circulate the results and ask the class to discuss them in the terms which were used for the texts in [2]. If it is possible to secure the comments of eleven-year-olds, they can be the basis for an additional session.

4] The aim of this session is to apply the class's new understanding of audience to the needs of the public examiner as an audience. Place questions from different examination levels, internal and external, side by side, for discussion, so that the class can explore what is appropriate to the examiner as an audience.

The goal of this unit is to show how a very familiar pattern in our vocabu
lary can reveal much about the attitude of our culture to what thos
words classify.

It takes as its starting point the fact that certain tasks are traditionally
thought to be the prerogative of one sex or the other, and goes on to
explore how the patterns of the vocabulary we use perpetuate thes
assumptions.

---

[1] The aim of this session is to discover which tasks in the household are
regarded as the man's job, and which the woman's. In discussion, con
sider such jobs as cooking, washing, washing-up, shopping, decorating
gardening, driving or washing the car, changing nappies, pushing the
pram or mending fuses.
The discussion should look at the position of brothers and sisters, as wel
as fathers and mothers, and consider to what extent tensions arise where
there is uncertainty as to who should do what within the family.

[2/3] The aim of these sessions is to show that a number of words in the
language carry with them the suggestion that particular jobs are properly
performed by one sex or the other, and thereby show that such additiona
meanings are an essential part of the way language determines how we
behave. This may be done in three ways:
    (a) by writing up the words Manager and Manageress, and asking the
        class to supply a list of organisations or institutions they may be
        found in charge of
    (b) by asking for examples of words which name jobs traditionally
        reserved for one sex, such as matron, au pair, jockey—or disc
        jockey. A variation of this is to write up a list of terms like 'con
        woman', 'charman' or 'nightwatchwoman' where the norma
        indications have been reversed
    (c) by asking for words like mayor which usually connote one sex, but
        may be the other, and exploring the linguistic difficulties that
        follow.

For this session, each member of the class should compile a list of names for jobs. By attempting to sort them into two simple lists, one clearly male, the other female, the class will discover that

(a) one term or the other has to be specially marked, as in doctor/ lady doctor or nurse/male nurse

(b) a similar job has different labels, as in Air Steward/Air Hostess

(c) some pairs have a missing term, as in -/fishwife, -/tomboy, or wide boy/-.

(d) in some related jobs, as in bus conductor/bus conductress and bus driver/-, a missing term may be significant.

The discussion will show how the resources of the language are exploited for this kind of labelling and consequently where the culture reveals itself in the gaps and special cases that occur.

• Related topics are explored in D7 and H6.

This unit is concerned with the relationship between diagrams and the language which is used to explain or supplement them.

It focuses upon the problems which arise when we try to convey information solely by diagram or solely by words, in order to explore the extent to which each can assist, and be dependent upon, the other.

---

[1] Ask the class to write a set of precise instructions, using words only, for an apparently very simple activity, of such a kind that the class would normally want to use a diagram at some stage during the writing. Have some of the accounts read aloud, and explore where and why the writers felt the need for diagrams.

Suitable activities include:

> *wiring up a*     *plug*
> *changing a*     *film in a camera*
> *changing a*     *typewriter ribbon*
> *setting up a*     *tape-recorder*

[2] For this session, ask the class to bring in a variety of instruction sheets which explain how to carry out simple operations, and use diagrams as well as words for the purpose. Organise the class in small groups and ask each group to take one of these, and re-write it so that the instructions given by diagrams are given only in words. Group discussion of text at each stage is necessary.

[3] Circulate the texts resulting from [2], and ask each group to point out in writing where and why the versions without diagrams are not clear. Give the original authors time to study the comments and then focus a class discussion upon the general points that arise.

[4] For this session, the class require versions of simple instruction-sheets from which the verbal matter has been deleted. Give one such version to each group and ask it to supply the missing verbal material. The complete text should be available for subsequent comparison with the class's attempt to supply it.

The instruction sheets found with cardboard cut-out models, dress patterns, plastic model kits, or in do-it-yourself manuals provide material to select from.

• Related topics are explored in A1, A7 and A10.

126

# National characteristics

This unit considers the extent to which our most firmly held assumptions about the world are often bound up with our use of common words, because the assumptions become attached to the words, and we acquire the words unreflectingly through their presence in our language.

It takes the particular example of our words for people of different nationalities and explores the ways in which they determine how we think of other nations, because their use carries with it assumptions we have never examined.

---

] The aim of the first session is to get the class to provide their own interpretations of common labels for nationalities. Divide the class into small groups each with a reporter who will require a grid, each column across labelled with the name of a nationality and each line down with a common characteristic. The reporter notes which characteristics his group assigns to each nationality.

The nationalities should include at least one from the U.K., one from the Commonwealth, and one from each continent. The characteristics can be such things as easy-going, well-dressed, religious, highly emotional, ill-mannered, unsporting.

] This session begins with each reporter announcing his group's decisions, which are recorded on the board, so as to build up a composite class picture for each nationality. The next stage is to ask the class how they knew what characteristics to assign to each nationality.

Questions like:

(a) has anyone visited these countries?

(b) has anyone met people from them?

(c) has anyone seen film or T.V. about them?

will help to focus the discussion upon any discrepancy between what the labels imply and what people are really like.

This session extends the inquiry by looking at a stereotyped written description. The object is to explore the ways in which such stereotypes come to be passed on by comics, fiction, television, film, theatre or radio. W. E. Johns, Alistair Maclean and Ian Fleming are the sort of writers who will provide the type of figure required.

[4] The class return to their original groups to prepare and perform a short dramatic sketch which makes use of a stereotype that the class as a whole are asked to identify.

- As an alternative to [4], or in addition, short stories can be written around a stereotype and circulated for class discussion.
- F3 enables the exploration to be taken further by examining those words that are used pejoratively or affectionately to refer to people of different nationality.

128